# FLOWER POWER
# PAPERCRAFTS

## 50 CARDS & GIFTS BLOSSOMING WITH FLORAL MOTIFS

### JULIE HICKEY

D&C
David and Charles

www.mycraftivity.com

A DAVID & CHARLES BOOK
Copyright © David & Charles Limited 2008

David & Charles is an F+W Media Inc. company
4700 East Galbraith Road
Cincinnati, OH 45236

First published in the UK and US in 2008

Text and projectdesigns copyright © Julie Hickey 2008
Photography copyright © David & Charles Limited 2008

Julie Hickey has asserted her right to be identified as author of this
work in accordance with the Copyright, Designs and Patents Act,
1988.

A catalogue record for this book is available from the British Library.

ISBN-13: 978-0-7153-2868-2 hardback
ISBN-10: 0-7153-2868-9 hardback

ISBN-13: 978-0-7153-2867-5 paperback
ISBN-10: 0-7153-2867-0 paperback

Printed in Singapore by KHL Printing Co Pte Ltd
for David & Charles
Brunel House      Newton Abbot      Devon

Commissioning Editor: Jennifer Fox-Proverbs
Desk Editor: Emily Rae
Project Editor: Jo Richardson
Art Editor: Charly Bailey
Production Controller: Ros Napper
Photographer: Ginette Chapman

Visit our website at www.davidandcharles.co.uk

David & Charles books are available from all good bookshops;
alternatively you can contact our Orderline on 0870 9908222 or
write to us at FREEPOST EX2 110, D&C Direct, Newton Abbot,
TQ12 4ZZ (no stamp required UK only); US customers call 800-
289-0963 and Canadian customers call 800-840-5220.

# CONTENTS

Introduction                          4
Choosing Floral Papers                6
Choosing Floral Embellishments        8

# CONTEMPORARY CHIC    10

# FLORAL FAIRIES        30

# FUNKY FLOWERS         50

# TRUE ROMANCE          70

# VINTAGE VOGUE         90

Basic Tool Kit                        110
Basic Techniques                      111
Decorating and Making Envelopes       114
Templates                             116
Materials                             118
Suppliers and About the Author        120
Acknowledgments and Index             121

# INTRODUCTION

We all lead such busy, hectic lives, so finding the time to create a unique card or papercrafted gift genuinely expresses what your friends and loved ones mean to you. The card or gift not only makes them feel extra special when they receive it, but they are far more likely to keep it over the years to come because you have put a part of you into it. I also find card- and gift-making wonderfully therapeutic, so papercrafting offers great benefits to the papercrafter too.

I have always loved paper and card, as well as flowers, so this book has given me the perfect excuse to play with all of the things I love most. When I'm making a card for a family member or friend, I always try to incorporate something they like, be it their favourite colour or flower. You can do the same with the many stunning floral papers, flower stamps and flower embellishments to choose from. And with the use of punches, die-cutting systems and templates, combined with sparkly crystals, gorgeous ribbons and fabulous buttons, you can create a multitude of beautiful blooms to adorn your cards and gifts, as you will see from the projects in this book. In addition to using a variety of craft techniques such as stamping, heat- and relief-embossing and découpage, the projects feature an array of materials, including metal, wire and acetate.

My aim is also to light an extra creative spark in you, perhaps with a certain flower, colour combination or layout, which you can use to bring something of your own to the projects.

# ABOUT THE BOOK

In the pages that follow, I give you some advice about how to choose floral papers and embellishments. The book is then split into five, very distinctly themed chapters – Contemporary Chic, Floral Fairies, Funky Flowers, True Romance and Vintage Vogue – which open with **Get the Look**, focusing on the particular colour combinations and elements that characterize each of them. For instance, it's the use of soft, subtle and muted tones that defines the Vintage Vogue look, in contrast to the bright, vibrant colours that say Contemporary Chic or Funky Flowers. Each chapter offers projects for a mixture of special occasions, from birthdays to anniversaries, ending in a **Blossoming Ideas** section that features additional designs to mark yet more events, together with schemes for decorating the insides of the cards or envelopes for a fully coordinated effect. The main projects within each theme include a quick and easy card and then a standard card and two 3-D projects, with the standard and 3-D projects featuring a variation that is a speedier, simpler take on the key design, often for an alternative occasion, and/or puts any leftover materials to creative use.

You'll also find a **Floral Focus** for each project, which highlights how and why I have used that particular floral element and suggestions for ways in which the look could be varied by changing it – in style, shape or colour. Additionally, I have explained the reasons behind my choice of layout, colour, technique and other embellishments in the **Creative Choices** that accompany the main projects, along with ideas for equally effective alternatives. The **You Will Need** lists itemize all of the specific tools and materials required, over and above the **Basic Tool Kit** on page 110, and full details of materials and suppliers are given at the back of the book on pages 118–120, as well as the templates needed on pages 116–117. This final section of the book also includes a demonstration of the core techniques that are involved in making most of the projects, together with guidance on decorating and making envelopes.

# CHOOSING FLORAL PAPERS

Design and colour are the key considerations when choosing papers for
your cards and gift projects, but equally important is actually whether or not
you like them – working with papers that you don't personally like will only
detract from your pleasure in papercrafting. I have to confess that when I
buy patterned papers I usually buy two sheets, one to use and one just to
look at and stroke. That way, once I have used a paper I really like I still have
it to keep, and I know this will make sense to a lot of other papercrafters
too. These pages show a selection of some floral papers that will work for
the different themes featured in the book.

## DESIGN

You will need to take into account how you are
going to use a floral paper in the selection process.
For instance, sometimes I choose a certain design
because I love its small pattern and know it will work
well when using a template to cut out and create
flowers or other motifs, as you will still be able to
see the pattern – see Easter Egg Trinity, page 28. On
the other hand, I may want to create an all-over
background for a project, such as the 21st Birthday
Bag, pages 20–23, so a larger-scale design would be
more appropriate because you will see more of it.
There are many stylized floral patterns available,
which come in a huge selection of colours. But if a
project calls for a more naturalistic flower design and
you can't find what you want, try creating your own
collection of papers. Use rubber stamps and colour in
the design with watercolour paints, pencils or chalks,
or use coloured inkpads to stamp your designs to
coordinate with your other decorative elements.
Some patterns are perfect for cutting out the flower
motifs and featuring them as a focal embellishment. I
also like to use punches (upside down so that I can
see where I'm punching) to cut out particular, eye-
catching elements from patterned papers. Try using
daisy, circle, tag and heart punches in this way.
Double-sided papers can be useful, with a different
but coordinated pattern and/or colour on each side
of the sheet. These are especially effective to use
when creating flowers, because if you curl and shape
the petals, seeing a little of the reverse/alternative
design or colour of the paper will add extra interest
to the blooms.

# WEIGHT

This can be an important consideration if the paper is to be used in a particular way. For instance, the paper stamped with a floral design and used to make envelopes for the Fairy's Secret Greetings booklet, pages 44–47, needs to be quite lightweight so that when it is scored and folded it lays nicely and gives crisp, neat edges – much harder to achieve with a heavyweight paper.

# SPECIAL FINISHES

Some floral patterns are printed onto shimmer paper, which will give a luxurious finish to your cards. You can also get papers that are pre-glittered and some that even come with floral elements in velvet flocking. Most papers are acid- and lignin-free, so can be used in scrapbooking projects, as they won't cause any deterioration to your precious photos. The only ones to avoid in this respect are glittered papers.

# CUTTING, EMBOSSING AND TEARING

You can cut floral papers with decorative scissors, such as scalloped-edged scissors, to give a shaped pattern to the edges, or die-cut or punch any shape you like from them. Most printed papers have a white paper base, so if you emboss them or create a distressed finish by sanding them, they will reveal their white core, which can look fabulous. Tearing such paper will also result in a white edge – an ideal effect for some projects.

# EMBELLISHING

Specialist pens are great for enhancing floral papers. Try glitter, gel, enamel or matt-finish pens to highlight different areas or patterns. A white pen can be used to add interesting details to dark-coloured paper. Trace some of the pattern with a fine-tip glue pen, sprinkle with glitter, tap off the excess and you have just created your own glitter paper collection!

# CHOOSING FLORAL EMBELLISHMENTS

There is a wealth of ready-made floral embellishments available on the market, in different materials, shapes, sizes and every colour imaginable, and these can also be decorated in a number of ways, as shown on these pages. You can also create your own extra-special blooms in colours to coordinate with your card and patterned papers. Choosing a particular shape, style and shade of flower will help to reflect the theme or look that you want.

## READY-MADE FLOWERS

Paper flowers come in an array of styles, from convincingly naturalistic to bold and stylized. Gorgeous, intricate laser-cut flowers, also available in different styles, sizes and colours, can be used to add delicate floral accents to a card, either individually or in groups, or as decorative borders. There is also a huge variety of shop-bought die-cut flowers in different colour combinations and styles of bloom. They can be used just as they are, or you can decorate them – try stamping, adding an enamelled finish, relief-embossing, punching holes or colouring with inkpads or chalks. The decorative possibilities are almost endless! There are lots of tactile felt and velvet flowers around too.

## HAND-MADE FLOWERS

You can also die-cut your own flowers using a die-cutting system and dies, allowing you to select the design and size you want and to cut it from whatever card or paper you desire. I loved using the Cricut die-cutting system to create the Coming of Age Carnival card on pages 56–59 in the Funky Flowers section.

Punches also offer lots of choice in flower design, as they come in so many different shapes and sizes. You can combine more than one style or use a range of sizes of the same flower to create a group of blooms. Petal templates can also be used to cut out individual petal shapes from paper or fabric, which can then be glued together to form fabulous flowers.

You can make flowers just using ribbon and secure them in the centre with jewelled or patterned brads to hold the pieces together. Try looping ribbon into petal shapes, or use folded lengths of ribbon or even snipped pieces – each method will produce a lovely flower with its own special quality and appeal.

# EMBELLISHING

Whether ready-made or hand-made, any flower can be enhanced by filling the centre with a decorative element, such as a single or group of crystals; colourful buttons, which can be tied with thread; circles punched from patterned paper or coloured card; or tied ribbons. You can also punch holes in the centres of flowers, then layer onto another card or paper colour to show through the holes. To give flat paper blooms shape and dimension, stretch each petal over a smooth, round object, such as an embossing tool or a pen.

# THEMED FLOWERS

Within the different chapters of the book, I have selected certain styles of flower to get the theme across. **Contemporary Chic** features a clean and simple punched daisy shape in bright colours (see pages 16–19), and for an ultra-modern, stylish look for Christmas, I have embossed bold poinsettias cut from sheet metal (see pages 24–27). In **Floral Fairies**, tiny punched daisies provide a decorative edging for the centrepiece of a mobile (see pages 40–43). By contrast, the die-cut blooms used to embellish a tweenie's envelope booklet are suitably fun and vibrant in hot pink and lilac (see pages 44–47). Die-cut flowers also set the punchy pace in **Funky Flowers**, here as dramatic silhouettes with cutout petals, which match the see-through quality of an acetate card (see pages 56–59). And big and bold shop-bought die-cuts, decorated with a relief pattern, feature as cut flowers (see pages 60–63). For **True Romance**, I have used both a traditional-styled rose stamp and a modern design (see pages 80–83). I have also embellished an accordion wedding book with sumptuous frilly-petalled pink and gold blooms cut using a template (see pages 84–87). In **Vintage Vogue**, I have used flower stickers in soft, muted shades that look like watercolours (see pages 94–95), and chose ready-made velvet flowers for an anniversary notice board in a luminous turquoise, contrasting with a pink patterned background (see pages 104–107).

# CONTEMPORARY CHIC

# GET THE LOOK

The key to Contemporary Chic is the use of vibrant colours but those that are really fresh-looking, for example bright pinks and blues or citrus orange and lime green, often combined with a lightening white. The floral elements I've used are modern and stylized, creating bold shapes with clean outlines, and I've often teamed these with geometric patterns like stripes and spots in coordinating colours. Compositions are also heavy on structure, with strong verticals and horizontals, and materials such as plasma – ultra-thick frosted plastic – and sheet metal add another modern dimension.

**The small-scale design** of this gorgeous floral-patterned paper in zingy citrus colours makes it perfect for card-making. The paper would look especially effective with the centres of the flowers punched out.

**The colour contrast** in this paper makes a lively impact, particularly in the form of stripes. Whether they are vertical, horizontal or diagonal, stripes look great with floral accents. Spotted papers are also a good basic ingredient to use with floral embellishments.

**Bright, modern colours** are again a feature of this paper, but the pattern is much more open, letting in lots of clean white. Pull out one of the colours, say the turquoise, and add embellishments in that colour, such as flowers, ribbons and glitter glue.

**Flowers and stripes** combine wonderfully well in this paper, again in colours that are vibrant and fresh, although in a limited palette. The large spirals give the pattern energy and impact.

**These silhouette flowers**
in shiny silver and pink metal are just right for a fun, trendy look, especially with jewelled brads in the centres. You could layer them onto patterned papers so that the design fills the petals.

**These bold, spiky daisies**
look fabulous with their centres filled with crystals, tied ribbon or even threaded buttons.

**These stylized, monochromatic flowers**
come complete with foam pads on the back. Add to a hot pink or turquoise background for real impact.

**These smaller paper flowers**
are perfect for adding in clusters to your Contemporary Chic designs. Fill the centres with single or groups of crystals for that extra touch of sparkle.

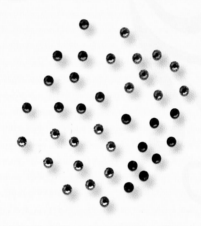

**Crystals make ideal flower centres**
for a finishing sparkle, available in a multitude of colours and sizes. I also use them in the corners of cards to help balance designs.

**These tiny paper flowers**
have tactile centres and fine stems. Attach the flower heads to your card, allowing the stems to hang down, or create a bunch of flowers. Alternatively, you could cut the stems off and use only the colourful flower heads.

**Use these vibrant flower sequins**
to create a stunning bouquet by arranging and gluing them in place. Add glitter glue or small brads to the centres.

**These stunning ribbons**
will make a quality contribution to any contemporary design: an orange, red and green woven floral ribbon; grosgrain ribbon in lime green with white polka dots; a satin ribbon printed with pink and green flowers; a wider-width pink sheer self-patterned ribbon.

# TAG TONIC

Give an ailing friend or family member an instant pick-me-up with this speedy but stylish get well card. The focal feature, a scallop-edged tag, is simply secured by threading through two slits that are cut into the horizontally striped paper before mounting onto the base card. Stylized paper flowers bring a softening contrast to the background pattern yet equal its bold impact, while crystals add a lifting sparkle.

## YOU WILL NEED

- ❀ pink and green striped paper
- ❀ green folded card, 14.8cm (6in) square
- ❀ white textured small scallop-top tag
- ❀ pale and deep pink paper flowers
- ❀ pink sheer striped ribbon
- ❀ pale pink crystals
- ❀ Basic Tool Kit (see page 110)

**1** Cut a piece of the striped paper 14.3cm (5½in) square. Using a craft knife against a metal-edged ruler, cut a slit approximately 4.5cm (1¾in) down from the top and 2.5cm (1in) across from the right-hand edge of the paper square long enough to accommodate the width of the tag. Cut a second slit 5.5cm (2¼in) from the top and 2.5cm (1in) from the same edge. Attach the paper to the folded card with double-sided tape.

**2** Create a double bloom by gluing a smaller pale pink flower to the centre of a larger deep pink flower. Attach to the card, overlapping the slits. Add a single pale pink flower below the double bloom.

**3** Thread the tag with the ribbon and tie in a knot. Insert the tag through the slits. Glue a single small deep pink flower to the tag alongside the pale pink flower. Glue crystals to the flower centres and in a horizontal row of three on the right-hand side of the tag.

## Floral Focus

Change the colour scheme to subdued lilacs and creams, using a single paper hydrangea flower head in a toning pastel shade, to create a soothing sympathy card.

# BIRTHDAY MEADOW

This lively, fabric-effect card will have wide appeal to female friends and relations of all ages to mark a special birthday, and it could easily be personalized by adding initials. Squares of pretty patterned papers are attached in a grid formation on the folded card, leaving a border in between, two having been embellished in different ways with ribbon ties. The edges are then zigzag-stitched in place using sparkling gold thread. Three punched pearlized card daisies punctuate the patchwork, their petals curled for an added element of dimension and their centres decorated with matching ribbon.

## Daisy Patches

Why not use up any scraps of paper and card left over from the main project to make a quick additional design for another birthday or as a thank you card, this time in a striking landscape format – the true crafter puts everything to creative use! A trio of differently patterned squares are layered onto card squares of varying colours and attached to the folded card in a horizontal row. A punched, shaped flower overlaps each square in differing positions.

## Floral Focus

The simple, stylized form of punched flowers is ideal for a bold, contemporary design, and there are lots of different styles to choose from. The centres are punched circles made to look like buttons, but you could use real buttons threaded with ribbon or fill the centres with crystals for a touch of bling!

## CREATIVE CHOICES

❀ The colours I chose are fresh and the patterns graphic, to give the design a modern yet decorative, feminine feel.

❀ The various floral-patterned papers work together harmoniously because they share the same tones and forms (drawn from one particular collection of papers), so don't be afraid to mix patterns.

❀ Positioning the flowers so that they overlap the edges of the squares serves to soften the strong lines of the design.

## YOU WILL NEED

❀ blue, orange, pink and green patterned papers in a selection of coordinating designs

❀ pastel blue folded card, 14.8cm (6in) square

❀ pearlized card – blue, green and pink

❀ narrow grosgrain ribbon – pastel blue, green and pink

❀ gold metallic thread

❀ punches – large daisy and small circle

❀ Basic Tool Kit (see page 110)

**1** Using a paper trimmer, cut a 4.5cm (1¾in) square from each of the different patterned papers. You will need nine squares in total.

Always trim ribbon at an angle to prevent it from fraying.

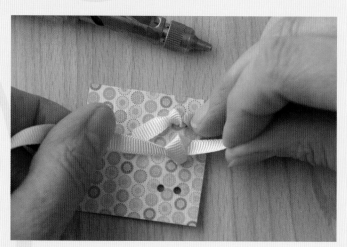

**2** To decorate one patterned paper square, using a Japanese screw punch, punch three sets of two holes, close together side by side, down the right-hand side. Thread each set of holes with a length of blue ribbon and tie in a knot. Trim the ends to the same length.

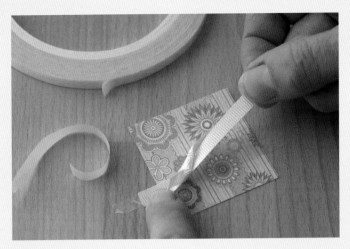

**3** For another paper square, cut a length of green ribbon slightly wider than the squares and tie a second length to it in a knot. Attach close to the bottom of the square with double-sided tape and trim the excess ribbon.

**4** Position the paper squares on the folded card front, leaving an even narrow border of card around each. Use a small amount of double-sided tape to secure the squares to the card. Using gold metallic thread, machine stitch around the edges of each with a row of zigzag stitches.

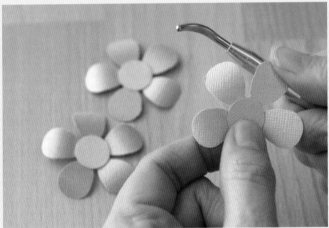

**5** Using the daisy punch, punch a single flower from the blue, green and pink pearlized card.

**6** Using the circle punch, punch a small circle from each of the pearlized card colours. Glue each circle to the centre of a matching-coloured daisy. Stretch each petal around a smooth, round object, such as an embossing tool or a pen, to curl.

**7** Using the Japanese screw punch, punch two holes in the centre of each flower. Thread with matching ribbon and tie in a knot. Trim the ribbon ends to the same length. Mount the flowers onto the card with foam pads.

# 21st Birthday Bag

Such a major birthday milestone deserves a suitably stylish gift package, and this boldly designed bag will really deliver, especially when filled with cellophane-wrapped, grown-up goodies. Printed papers are decoratively stitched together to create a sturdy front and back with a colour-coordinated lining and in-built ribbon side ties. Contrasting ribbon and rickrack handles tied with dangling die-cut flower charms and a gem-studded number tag complete the look. An extra feature is a front pocket for adding a matching card or tag with the recipient's name or initial.

## Floral Focus

This stylized floral motif is perfect for a modern 21 year old. For equally fashionable Valentine's Day or wedding anniversary gifts, use a contemporary-style rose motif and team it with a die-cut rose tag and charms.

## Well Tagged

Take the key elements of the bag design and make a lookalike, trendy tag-shaped card, which can be tucked into the pocket – striped paper for a panel, rickrack for a (glued-on) border and a foam pad-mounted flower charm, finished off with a bright pink checked ribbon tie.

## CREATIVE CHOICES

❀ Bright, funky colours and clean, simple shapes and detailing offer instant appeal to a young adult.

❀ I selected the floral and striped patterned papers from the same collection, so they effortlessly mix and match to great effect.

## YOU WILL NEED

❀ patterned papers – deep pink/lilac floral and deep pink/lilac striped

❀ linen card – lilac and deep pink

❀ deep pink ribbon

❀ rickrack – lilac and deep pink

❀ lilac sewing thread

❀ sheet of chipboard

❀ mini chipboard numbers '2' and '1'

❀ burgundy crystals

❀ scoreboard (optional)

❀ die-cutting system and flower and circles dies

❀ medium circle punch

❀ Basic Tool Kit (see page 110)

**1** Cut two pieces of floral paper 28 × 22cm (11 × 8¾in) for the bag front and back. Cut two pieces of striped paper the same size for the inside front and back. Using Gate 1 on the scoreboard, score along the top and bottom of all four pieces. If you don't have a scoreboard, score 2.5cm (1in) from the top and bottom edges with an embossing tool.

**2** Attach a length of ribbon to either side of the floral front and back pieces 7.5cm (3in) from the bottom edges. With wrong sides facing, attach the striped paper pieces to the floral paper pieces with double-sided tape in the centre, to hold in place. Using the lilac thread, machine stitch a row of zigzag stitches around the edges of both joined pieces, sandwiching the ribbon in between the layers.

**3** Cut a piece of striped paper 17.5 × 8.5cm (7 × 3½in) and machine stitch to the bottom centre of the bag front. Cut four strips of lilac card 28 × 2.8cm (11 × 1⅛in) and machine stitch either side of the pocket on the bag front and in the same position on the bag back. Machine stitch ribbon and then lilac rickrack down the centre of the lilac strips on the bag front and back, creating two loops at the top for handles.

**4** Cut a base from the chipboard sheet 8.5 × 22cm (3½ × 8¾in). Place a length of strong double-sided tape on the inside front of the bag along the bottom, just below the scored line. Pull away part of the backing paper from the tape, then position the chipboard base over the top, pull the backing paper away and press down to secure. Repeat to attach the base to the inside back of the bag. Cover the base top with floral paper and the base bottom, concealing where the front and backs attach, with striped paper. Fold along the score lines and tie the ribbon ties together.

**5** Glue the chipboard numbers to the striped paper, with the stripes running vertically on the '2' and horizontally on the '1'. Leave to dry, then trim the excess paper from around the edges with a craft knife.

Remember to face the numbers right-side down on the striped paper to ensure you cover the front rather than the back.

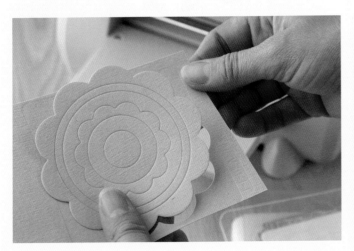

**6** Die-cut a flower shape from lilac card and lift the outer petals from the sheet. Die-cut a circle from pink card and attach to the back of the lilac petals to form a flower-shaped tag. Attach the numbers to the tag with foam pads. Decorate the numbers with crystals. Using a Japanese screw punch, punch a hole in the tag top, thread with pink rickrack and tie to the bag handle.

**7** For the flower charms, die-cut one smaller flower from lilac card and one from pink card, and die-cut a similar-sized circle from each card. Glue contrasting-coloured flowers and circles together. Punch a small circle from each card and glue to the charm centres, matching the colour with the petals. Decorate the centres with crystals. Using the Japanese screw punch, punch a hole in each petal. Thread a length of pink rickrack through a hole in each charm and knot the end, then tie the other end to the handle.

# SEASONAL SHIMMER

Surprise and delight family or friends with this trend-setting Christmas card, tailor-made to fit a CD tin. The lid provides a tantalizing foretaste of what's contained within – a pink circle layered on a contrasting ice blue scallop-edged circle, both die-cut from lustrous shimmer card and the latter decorated with punched holes for a doily-type effect, topped with a tied band of ribbon. The crowning glory is a flamboyant relief-embossed metal poinsettia flower, artily coloured with alcohol inks to coordinate with its backdrop. The tin opens to reveal three more such poinsettia-adorned discs in alternating colourways, strung together with ribbon ties, for a truly sumptuous seasonal greeting.

## Floral Focus

I chose a poinsettia flower, as it is customarily associated with Christmas, but I've given it an up-to-date twist by rendering it in modern metal and a non-traditional colour scheme. You could use a Christmas rose instead, or holly-leaf shapes.

## Clearly Christmas

For this unusual translucent design, two scallop acetate circles are edged with a permanent white inkpad, then a blue shimmer card circle attached with double-sided tape to the front and a pink scallop card circle attached to the reverse of the acetate circle, concealing the previously used tape. An embossed-metal poinsettia is mounted centrally onto the blue circle. A pink circle is then attached to the front of the back acetate circle, with a blue scallop circle on the reverse.

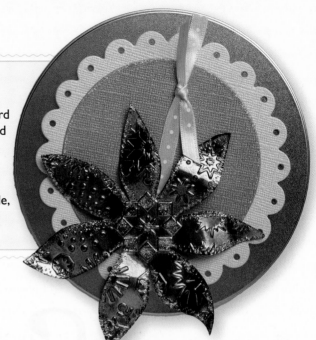

## CREATIVE CHOICES

❀ Pink and ice blue are unexpected choices for the festive season, but they work wonderfully together, both in the scallop-edged card circles and the inks used for colouring the metallic poinsettias, and create a high-impact effect.

❀ The combination of the simple, strong shape of the poinsettia flower and the scallop-edged circle helps to reinforce the clean, contemporary look, with the embossing of the metal adding subtle, textural embellishment.

## YOU WILL NEED

❀ CD tin

❀ shimmer card – ice blue and pink

❀ die-cut poinsettia flower

❀ self-adhesive silver metal sheet

❀ alcohol inks – blue and pink

❀ spotted pale blue narrow satin ribbon

❀ iridescent glitter glue

❀ die-cutting system and scallop and circle dies

❀ snowflake embossing folder for die-cutting system

❀ decorative embossing roller

❀ Basic Tool Kit (see page 110)

**1** Using the die-cutting system, die-cut four large scallop-edged circles, to fit inside the CD tin, three from ice blue shimmer card and one from pink shimmer card. Die-cut four smaller circles, three from the pink card and one from the ice blue card.

**2** Using a Japanese screw punch, punch a hole in the centre of each scallop shape around the edge of each die-cut scallop-edged circle.

**3** Lay the poinsettia flower on the back (adhesive side) of the metal sheet. Cut around the outside edge of the flower with a craft knife. Repeat to cut out a total of four poinsettia flowers from the metal sheet.

You could omit the poinsettia from the middle disc and use a stamped greeting instead, or add a family photo to the inner circle – a great way to connect with absent relatives across the miles at Christmas time.

**4** Place one of the poinsettia flowers in the embossing folder and run through the die-cutting system. Repeat with the remaining three flowers. Roll a decorative embossing roller over the edges of all the poinsettia flowers.

**5** Colour the embossed flowers with the alcohol inks by applying both inks to the applicator and dabbing all over the flower, then changing the direction of the applicator. This will give them a random colouring.

**6** Stretch the petals of each poinsettia flower over a smooth, round object, such as an embossing tool or a pen, to curl. Attach one centrally to the pink-edged blue circle with foam pads. Then attach one to two of the blue-edged pink circles off-centre and trim the overhanging petals. Link the three circles together in a row by threading each of two adjacent holes with a length of ribbon, knotting and trimming. Apply glitter glue around the edges of the flowers and leave to dry.

**7** Decorate the edge of the inner circle of the remaining scallop-edged card circle with glitter glue and leave to dry, then attach to the CD tin lid with double-sided tape. Tie two lengths of ribbon together, then attach across the centre of the circle with double-sided tape and trim off the excess. Mount the remaining poinsettia flower to the circle to the right of the ribbon tie, without trimming the overhanging petals, using foam pads.

# BLOSSOMING IDEAS

Cater for yet more celebratory occasions with these additional designs, including a matching tag and envelope, each with a quality, contemporary look that is sure to find favour with a wide variety of people.

## EASTER EGG TRINITY

Everyone loves an Easter egg, and this card offers a trio of pretty pink ones decorated mix-'n'-match-style. The two outer eggs cut from small floral-patterned paper feature a plain pink band cut with scallop-edged scissors, embellished with three daisies punched from the same patterned paper, with centres punched from pink checked paper. The middle egg, cut from the latter, is dotted all over with the same daisy decorations and topped with a pink grosgrain ribbon tied in a bow. Iridescent glitter glue adds sparkling highlights to the flower centres. The eggs are mounted onto a white landscape card with foam pads, for a touch of dimension.

### CREATIVE CHOICES
Patterned paper with an all-over small-scale pattern is needed for this design in order to work effectively on the cutout egg shapes, but you can vary the look by using different colour combinations of papers, such as lemon, pink and soft green, orange, yellow and lime green or yellow with lilac and soft green.

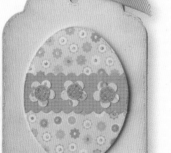

### BEAUTIFUL TAG
Create a coordinating tag to accompany a special Easter gift by mounting a floral-patterned egg, made in the same way as for the card, onto a white scallop-top tag with foam pads. Ink the edges of the tag with a deep pink inkpad, then thread with pink ribbon to match.

Always finish your card before adding glitter glue so that you can put it to one side to dry and not risk smudging it.

# WEDDING BANDS

Make a style statement with this cutting-edge wedding card design, which is sure to stand out from the crowd! The inside back of this trendy transparent acetate folded card features a square panel of floral-patterned paper, with a smaller plain orange square layered on top. This is smartly secured in place by a punched small orange daisy at each corner, which has two holes punched through the centre, as well as through the patterned paper panel and acetate beneath, threaded and tied with deep pink ribbon. A band of orange paper is glued to the card front, topped with a narrower band of the patterned paper, then embellished with a pink crystal outline heart and a pair of paper flowers with crystal centres.

### CREATIVE CHOICE
The deep pink and orange colour scheme I have used here is vibrant and striking in a particularly modern way, with the predominance of white keeping it fresh and not overpowering. Alternatively, you could choose another two colours that work well together which echo the bride's colours, if you know them.

## BEAUTIFUL OUTSIDE
This envelope is cut from the same floral paper used for the card (see page 116 for the template), and the front decorated with punched daisies, again secured in place with knotted ribbon threaded through two holes punched in each centre. Once the sides and bottom flap are folded where indicated on the template, and the back flap glued in place (see page 115), the top flap is sealed with an orange paper strip punched along one long edge with a corner rounder punch.

# FLORAL FAIRIES

# GET THE LOOK

To capture that enchanting Floral Fairy look, choose pretty pastel colours or, for a bolder effect, two-tone schemes in pinks and purples or yellows and oranges, but in any case you want lots of magical glitz and glitter. You can opt for sparkle paper or add glitter glue details or loose glitter to ordinary patterned paper. Colour in stamped fairy images with glitter gel pens, and use jewelled brads and crystals for eye-catching highlights. I chose flowers with cutout petals especially for their airy quality, but also used shimmer inkpads to stamp a floral design and created a delicate, almost lacy effect with lots of tiny punched flowers. Ribbon trimmings add the perfect finishing flourish.

**The soft pastel papers below**
immediately suggest a light and airy feel, which couldn't be more appropriate for the fairy theme. The paper far right comes with glitter on it, but you can always embellish any standard-finish shop-bought papers by applying either loose glitter or glitter glue in iridescent or a specific matching or coordinating colour.

**Delicate, laser-cut daisies and frilled flowers**
come in different sizes, colours and designs. They are fabulous for sprinkling among images of fairies on cards. You could try adding glitter to the centres too. Simply snip them from the sheet, either individually or in a strip to use as an instant border.

**Paper flowers in pastel shades**
and a variety of sizes look stunning with
spangly crystals added to their centres.
Try double-layering them, attaching a
smaller one inside a larger one, to create
showy double blooms.

**These flowers with cutout petals**
have a lovely light, dainty quality, in spite
of their relatively large size, which is
perfect for conveying a fairy feel. To make
them even more decorative, fill the petals
with patterned papers. Or use acetate,
cover it with glue and sprinkle with loose
glitter for super sparkly fairy flowers.

**These pretty die-cut flowers,**
available in a variety of shapes, sizes
and colours, can be easily enhanced by
curling the petals for a 3-D look. Try
edging the petals with glitter glue or
colouring them with chalks or inkpads.
Fill the centres with punched patterned
papers, buttons or tied ribbons.

**These flower-shaped brads**
in two different sizes and various bright
colours will add delightful decorative
detail to your fairy designs. Depending
on use, you may need to cover the
back with a strip of patterned paper or
coloured card to hide the brad 'wings'.

**Opulent jewelled brads,**
pictured here in two different
sizes and assorted colours, also
come square-shaped. Add to
the centres of flowers or use to
attach a panel of paper to a card
with one in each corner.

**These dainty daisy eyelets**
have separate yellow eyelets for their
centres. Attach to your card and add
ribbon stems to them. They would
look lovely along the bottom of card
with a fairy figure above.

**Choose one of these ribbons**
to finish off your fairy designs in feminine style:
pale turquoise satin ribbon with tiny spots;
lilac sheer ribbon printed with white spots;
soft pink sheer ribbon with a self stripe; daisy-
shaped ribbon with coloured centres.

# BIRTHDAY GIRL'S FAIRYTALE

Make a little girl's birthday wishes come true with this magical card design featuring a playful pair of 3-D fairy figures. The base card is formed of two scalloped card squares, their edges highlighted with ink, then punched and tied together with ribbon. The bodies of the découpage fairies are double layered and mounted onto the card with foam pads for extra dimension, then decorated with glitter glue. Clusters of die-cut flowers embellish two corners of the card squares.

## YOU WILL NEED

* 2 white scallop-edged card squares, 12.5cm (5in)
* card – yellow and orange
* orange inkpad
* satin ribbon – spotted orange and yellow
* floral fairies découpage sheets
* topaz crystals
* iridescent glitter glue
* die-cutting system and flower shapes die
* Basic Tool Kit (see page 110)

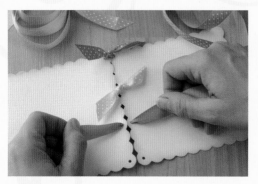

**1** Ink the edges of the card squares with the orange inkpad. Using a Japanese screw punch, punch four evenly spaced holes down the right-hand side of one square. Repeat with the other square by placing the punched square on top and punching through the holes so that they are exactly aligned. Lay the squares side by side, with the punched edges adjacent to each other. Thread each adjacent set of holes with a length of ribbon, alternating the colours, tie in a knot and trim to an even length.

**2** Push two of the same standing fairies from the découpage sheets, then cut out the body only of the second fairy and layer onto the first fairy using foam pads. Repeat with a sitting fairy. Mount the fairies onto the card squares with foam pads.

**3** Using the die-cutting system, die-cut different-sized flower shapes from the yellow and orange card. Glue to opposing corners of the card squares. Add crystals to the flower centres, using a group of three for the largest flower. Decorate the fairies and their wings with glitter glue, then leave to dry.

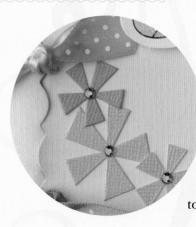

## Floral Focus

These cute, clean-cut and contemporary-style découpage fairies need some stylized flower shapes to complement them, and these bold, angular-shaped die-cut examples fill the part perfectly, and are colour-matched to their dresses and hair.

# FESTIVE FAIRY

A Christmas fairy is always a firm favourite with adults and children alike, and here she springs from a sparkling snowflake backdrop, wired for festive fun – literally! Both have been created using stamps, but our flying friend has been brought to life by being cut out and coloured in, wire and punched details attached, and mounted onto a fancy-edged tag to create a fabulous 3-D feature. Crystals and glitter glue add just the right touch of seasonal sparkle.

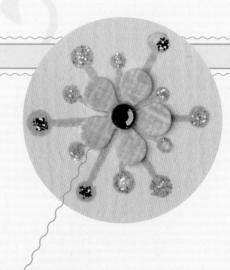

## Floral Focus

Specially chosen for their flowery feel, these stamped snowflakes are given an extra boost of flower power by adding punched daisies and spangly crystal centres.

## Fairy Garland Tag

The fairy tag alone would make a magical addition to any gift. For an even quicker effect, simply stamp and colour in the fairy straight onto the tag, but make and add the sparkling floral garland as described in Step 5, page 39. Icy, pastel shades of pink, green and purple would look pretty applied to the design instead of blue, as shown.

## CREATIVE CHOICES

❀ I replaced the stamped fairy's standard stick arms and legs with wire ones, winding the legs into spirals for a fun 'twist', and crowning her head with a wire halo.

❀ Cool, frosty tones of ice blue, silver and white chosen for the colour scheme give a wintry yet glamorous feel that's perfect for Christmas.

## YOU WILL NEED

❀ white textured folded card, 14.8 x 10.5cm (6 x 4in), plus extra for stamping and punching

❀ white textured small scallop-top tag

❀ stamps – snowflakes in 2 sizes and fairy

❀ inkpads – blue and permanent black

❀ 22-gauge silver wire

❀ shimmer paints – pale yellow, turquoise and bright blue

❀ blue crystals

❀ spotted blue satin ribbon

❀ aqua glitter glue

❀ paintbrush

❀ waterbrush (optional)

❀ punches – medium and tiny daisies

**1** Using the blue inkpad, randomly stamp snowflakes in two different sizes all over the folded card front, printing some over the edges of the card.

Stamping some motifs over the edges of the card adds a professional touch, keeping the design balanced.

**2** Using the black inkpad, stamp the fairy onto white textured card. Cut around the outline, cutting off the arms and legs. Cut out the hands and feet, and set aside.

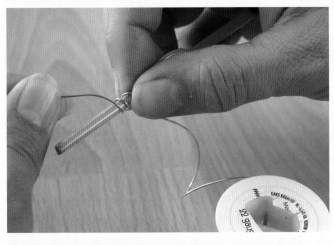

**3** Create a halo by bending a short length of wire around your finger and twisting the ends together to secure. Bend another short length of wire into a 'V' shape for arms. Curl another two short lengths around a paintbrush handle to create spiral legs. Glue the feet to the ends of the legs with craft glue.

**4** Using a waterbrush or wet paintbrush and the shimmer paints, colour in the fairy, including the hands and feet, then leave to dry. Attach the halo to the back of the fairy's head with double-sided tape. Cut a slit on either side of the fairy's body with a craft knife and thread the arms through. Glue the hands to the ends. Attach the legs to the back of the dress with double-sided tape.

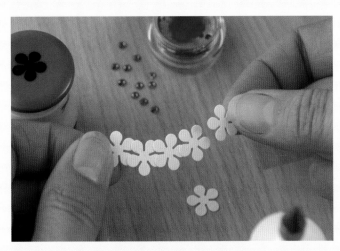

**5** Using the medium daisy punch, punch six daisies from white textured card. Glue together to create a garland. Colour in with the shimmer paints, then leave to dry. Glue a crystal to each flower centre, then glue the garland to the fairy's hands.

**6** Use the blue inkpad to ink the edges of the tag, then leave to dry. Thread a length of ribbon through the tag. Tie the end of a second length of ribbon to the end of the first ribbon that emerges from the front of the tag and knot to secure. Attach the remaining free lengths of ribbon vertically to the card with double-sided tape, trimming level with the top and bottom edges. Secure the tag to the card and mount the fairy onto the tag with foam pads.

**7** Punch medium and tiny daisies from white textured card, then colour in with the blue shimmer paint and leave to dry. Glue to the centres of the stamped snowflakes. Glue crystals to the centres of the medium daisies. Highlight the snowflakes, fairy and tag edges, and also fill the centres of the daisies, with the glitter glue. Leave to dry.

# DAISY-CHAIN MOBILE

Bring a little fairy magic into a baby's early view of the world with this delightfully delicate, flower-festooned mobile. The star attraction is assembled from cutout card and paper shapes, then mounted onto an oval card panel, all decorated with tiny punched flowers. Cutout-petalled flowers, with punched circle and flower centres, add a suitably airy dimension. A chipboard hanger and hearts are covered with pretty pastel patterned paper, the latter again decorated with punched flowers, then threaded with coordinating ribbon, on which all the various decorative elements are strung.

## Floral Focus

The tiny punched daisies work ideally for this modern-look fairy, but using the same template, you could cut her dress from floral-patterned paper instead for a traditional feel or decorate a gingham-checked dress with dainty fabric flowers for a more country effect.

## Hovering Hanger

Make an enchanting door hanger for the new baby's room from the papers and flowers left over from the mobile. The fairy is made in the same way, but here the wings have been embellished all over with punched flowers. Larger punched flowers form a decorative border, and a scallop-edged circle of patterned paper frames the hole. You could personalize the hanger with the baby's name or just her initial, or make it a wonderful gift to mark a first birthday by adding a number '1'.

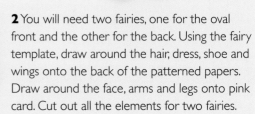

**YOU WILL NEED**

❀ card – yellow and pink

❀ white sparkle paper

❀ coordinating patterned papers

❀ yellow glitter glue

❀ 3 chipboard hearts and hanger

❀ pink and yellow flowers with cutout petals – 3 large and 8 medium

❀ ribbon – pink medium grosgrain; yellow and pink narrow satin

❀ oval shape-cutter

❀ fairy plastic template

❀ punches – tiny, medium and large daisy; medium and small circle

❀ Basic Tool Kit (see page 110)

**1** Choose an oval template for the cutter that will fit the fairy within it with room to spare. Cut out from yellow card. Punch tiny daisies from the white sparkle paper. Glue around the oval edge on both sides. Dot the glitter glue in the flower centres and leave to dry.

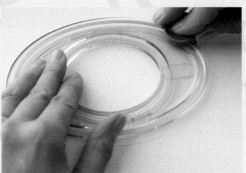

**2** You will need two fairies, one for the oval front and the other for the back. Using the fairy template, draw around the hair, dress, shoe and wings onto the back of the patterned papers. Draw around the face, arms and legs onto pink card. Cut out all the elements for two fairies.

Remember to turn the template over when drawing around the arm and leg shapes so that you have a left and right of each.

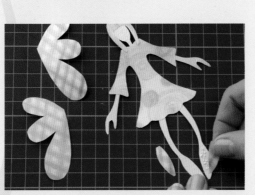

**3** Assemble the two fairies by gluing the hair onto the face, then attach the dress and glue the arms to the backs of the sleeves. Glue patterned paper shoes to the legs, then attach the legs to the back of the dress along the bottom. Decorate the dress with tiny daisies punched from white sparkle paper. Fill the centres with glitter glue and leave to dry.

**4** Apply thick craft glue to one side of each chipboard heart, lay patterned paper on top and press down firmly to adhere. Leave to dry for about 10 minutes. Trim the excess paper around each heart using a craft knife. Cover the other side of each heart and trim in the same way. Decorate both sides of the hearts with medium daisies punched from white sparkle paper. Fill the centres with glitter glue and leave to dry.

**5** Decorate both sides of the large cutout flowers with medium circles punched from patterned paper and the smaller flowers with small punched circles. Punch a large daisy for each flower centre from white sparkle paper and stretch the petals over a smooth, round object, such as an embossing tool or a pen, to curl. Glue to the patterned paper circles on one side of each flower. Fill the flower centres with glitter glue and leave to dry. Repeat for the other sides of the flowers.

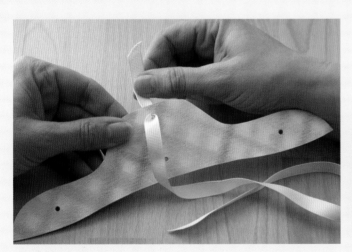

**6** Apply thick craft glue to one side of the chipboard hanger, lay patterned paper on top and press down firmly to adhere. Leave to dry for about 10 minutes. Trim the excess paper around the hanger using a craft knife. Using a Japanese screw punch, punch a hole in the top of the hanger and three evenly spaced holes along its length. Thread a length of the grosgrain ribbon through the top hole and knot the ends together to hang the mobile.

**7** Punch a hole in the centre of each heart and another at the bottom. Punch a hole in the top and bottom of the oval. Thread yellow ribbon through the left-hand hole in the hanger and tie in a single knot to secure. Tie the other end to the top of a smaller decorated cutout flower. Tie another length to the bottom of the flower, then thread through the centre hole in the heart and out through the bottom hole. Tie the end to another smaller cutout flower. Tie pink narrow ribbon to the centre hole of the hanger, then thread through a heart and tie to the top of the oval. Tie another length to the bottom hole, then tie to a large cutout flower. Thread the remaining hole in the hanger in the same way as the first. Decorate the front and back of the hanger with cutout flowers.

# FAIRY'S SECRET GREETINGS

Looking for a way to wow your favourite tweenie? This ribbon-bound booklet is especially designed to surprise and entrance her, each page of which is actually a delightful fairy-and-flower-stamped envelope containing a card tag. These are decorated to coordinate with the envelopes with stamped fantastical toadstools, fluttering butterflies and yet more enchanting fairies, together with die-cut flowers, a double one secured in the centre with a jewelled brad attached to a scallop-edged circle providing a tab for pulling out the tag. The white fairy panels offer plenty of space for adding messages and/or photos, to personalize the present.

## Floral Focus

The clean, simple shapes of the die-cut flowers echo the style of the stamped flower design, to give a nicely unified look, even though there are lots of elements in play here. And one of the fairy designs features another, similarly bold flower – a gorgeous giant gerbera daisy, also used in the quick card project left and below.

## Giant Gerbera Greeting

You can make this stunning birthday card as a speedy option using just two of the stamp designs. A wide band of white card is randomly stamped with the flower design in pink, layered onto wider bright pink card trimmed with scallop-edged scissors and glued to the folded card, then embellished with tied deep pink ribbon. The fairy is stamped onto white card and a circle die-cut around her, then layered over a die-cut scallop-edged pink card circle, which is attached to the card with foam pads. Glitter glue highlights give her appropriate sparkle.

## CREATIVE CHOICES

❋ I chose a lively colour scheme of hot pink and lilac/purple to have an especially strong appeal to aspiring teenagers, but making it just two tone with a fresh white background prevents the action-packed design from being overly busy.

❋ Using glitter gel pens is a great way of adding glamorous sparkle to the stamped fairy designs as you colour them in.

## YOU WILL NEED

❋ A4 (US letter) white paper

❋ card – white, pink and lilac

❋ stamps – flowers, 2 fairies, toadstools and butterflies

❋ inkpads – shimmer purple, shimmer pink and black permanent

❋ pink and purple jewelled brads

❋ glitter gel pens

❋ pink crystals

❋ ribbon – white spotted pink and purple, pink and lilac

❋ envelope template

❋ scoreboard

❋ scallop-edged scissors

❋ die-cutting system and flower dies

❋ punches – corner rounder and scallop-edged circle

❋ Basic Tool Kit (see page 110)

You could add a name or numbers to celebrate a special birthday, such as '13', to the front of the booklet to personalize it in a more up-front way.

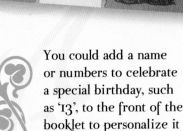

**1** Randomly stamp the flower design all over a sheet of white paper using a shimmer purple inkpad. Stamp another two sheets of white paper in the same way, then stamp two more sheets with a shimmer pink inkpad.

**2** On the reverse of one of the sheets of stamped paper, trace around the envelope template and cut out. Score along the fold lines using a scoreboard. Fold along the score lines and glue the envelope together. Repeat with the other stamped sheets of paper to make another four envelopes.

**3** Stamp the two different fairies onto white card using a black permanent inkpad, stamping five for the envelopes and five for the tags. Leave to dry. Trim the stamped panels to 10 x 5.5cm (4 x 2¼in). Trim the long edges of six slightly wider card panels, five of pink and five of lilac, with scallop-edged scissors, then layer the stamped panels on top.

**4** Using a die-cutting system, die-cut flowers for the envelopes and tags. For the small flowers, die-cut a flower from lilac and pink card, then glue together. Create large blooms by layering three die-cut flowers from the same coloured card together.

**5** Cut tags from pieces of card 10 x 18cm (4 x 7in), three in pink and two in lilac. Shape the corners using a corner rounder punch. Punch a scallop-edged circle for each tag from the contrasting card colour. Die-cut a double bloom for each scallop-edged circle in the card colour to match the tag and attach to the centre of each circle with a jewelled brad.

**6** Stamp the tags with toadstools and butterflies using the black inkpad. Attach a fairy-stamped panel to the front of each envelope and to each tag, contrasting the colours, using double-sided tape. Colour in the images with glitter gel pens and leave to dry. Attach the flowers to the envelopes and tags, with the scalloped-circle flower overlapping the right-hand edge of the tag. Add a crystal to the centre of each smaller flower to finish

**7** Score down the left-hand edge of all the envelopes. Using a Japanese screw punch, punch holes at evenly spaced intervals down the spine. Layer the envelopes together, alternating the colours, using double-sided tape. Thread each set of holes with a length of ribbon, alternating the colours down the spine, and tie to secure.

# BLOSSOMING IDEAS

Floral-enhanced fairies are the perfect messengers when you want to convey a sincere sentiment, whether it's to wish someone a speedy convalescence or to send them heartfelt thanks. So spread their special magic yet further with these delightful designs.

## UPLIFTING SPIRIT

This flower-bearing fairy is on a dedicated mission to bring some charmed cheer to aid a loved one in their recovery from illness. A transparent plasma flower shape is backed with two pieces of purple card cut to match, then strung together at the top with purple ribbon threaded through a punched hole. A die-cut circle of white card is glued to the centre of the plasma, then stamped with the fairy figure and coloured in with watercolour pencils, a second layer being added to the dress and wings. Purple paper flowers with crystal centres frame the focal image, with one for the fairy to hold. More crystals and glitter glue give her extra glitz.

### CREATIVE CHOICE
I used ready-made paper flowers to edge the central circle of card, since they instantly add texture and dimension, but to vary the look, you could punch flowers from patterned paper and use in the same way.

**BEAUTIFUL OUTSIDE**

Why not add to the recipient's delight by making a decorative liner for the envelope to match the fairy card design. Here, pearlized purple paper is stamped all over with a simple daisy design using a black inkpad, then glued inside a ready-made white envelope.

The simplest way to fit the envelope liner is to cut the paper to the overall width and height of envelope, with the flap open. After stamping with the motif, glue to the inside of the envelope and flap, then trim around the flap.

# FAIRY'S THANK YOU

No one can resist a secret message, and this fun design incorporates a little personal note of thanks written on pearlized paper, rolled up and disguised as a flower stem! The flower head is formed from two different-sized paper flowers secured together in the centre with a jewelled brad. Two sets of holes are punched in the card front, wide enough apart to accommodate the rolled-up note, ribbon threaded through and tied around the 'stem' to secure. The fairy is stamped onto white card, cut out and coloured in with glitter gel pens, then attached to the card using foam pads, with a crystal flower glued to her wand. Two lengths of ribbon in toning colours are tied together and secured in place with double-sided tape.

Instead of a message, you could roll up a banknote and use as the flower stem instead – a great way to give a card and cash gift in one go!

### CREATIVE CHOICES

The big double flower, with its chunky stem and jewelled centre, makes a dramatic impact, but the stamped fairy draws her fair share of attention by being coloured with eye-catching glitter gel pens. The limited colour palette serves to unify the design as a whole.

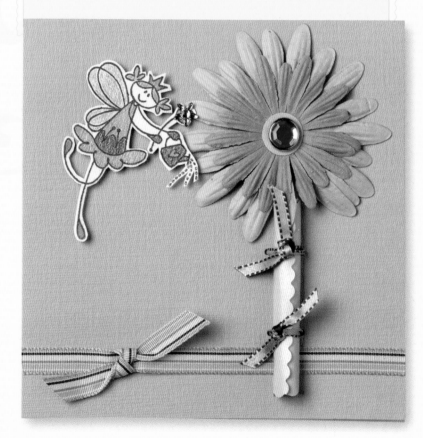

# FUNKY FLOWERS

# GET THE LOOK

Bright and bold is what Funky Flowers says to me, with dramatic colour contrasts such as orange and black, more surprising combinations like pinky browns and greens or a multicoloured vibrant mix. The floral elements I've used are equally high on impact – simple, strong die-cut or punched shapes or chunky-petalled, ready-made blooms. To heighten the effect further, I've also put an emphasis on texture, not just textured papers but flowers relief-embossed with an all-over pattern, chipboard numbers heat-embossed to a rich, glossy finish or paper panels stitched with coloured thread. I've gone for strong patterning too, with pretty paisley-printed background papers and spotted ribbon and buttons for eye-catching flower centres.

**With their unconventional colour combinations** and patterns, the two papers below are full of impact even though they are relatively dark in tone, which makes them just right for the Funky Flowers look. The vertically lined design could be cut into strips and used to mimic patterned ribbon. Apply glitter glue to the flower centres to really lift the motifs from the background.

**This powerful pink paper** with different-sized funky-shaped flower heads in shades of the single colour would make a great all-over background for a card. Alternatively, you could cut the flowers from the sheet to give your card or papercrafted gift its floral focus.

**Tactile deep embossing** is the characteristic element of this unusual floral-patterned paper. A strip of this down the edge of a card with a simple ribbon-tied message would make a quick and easy yet highly stylish card.

**Glossy enamel-effect florals**
in stark black and white contrasting
colours and bold patterns would look
simply stunning added to a hot fuchsia
pink card.

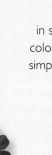

**These stitched suede flowers**
will give a warm, fuzzy feel to your cards and
add unexpected visual interest and dimension.
Why not extend the stitching element and sew
buttons to the centres in coordinating thread.

**These frilly-textured blooms**
in wild colours will definitely give
impact to your cards. Big, bright, shiny
buttons in the centres will finish the
effect perfectly.

**Buttons in bright colours**
make ideal decorative details for
Funky Flowers designs, pictured here
in spotty, matt, clear and glittered
forms. Add thread or ribbon to
their centres in coordinating or
contrasting hues.

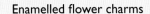

**Enamelled flower charms**
with their well-defined, light-catching
edges can be tied onto a card with
ribbon or thread, or even with a
thin strip of coloured card.

**In coloured translucent acrylic,**
these flowers would look especially
effective added to a bold stamped
design, bringing it texture and
dimension. Alternatively, draw stems
onto card with a glitter gel pen and
add the flowers to the top.

**Use these zany ribbons and braid**
to add a finishing funky element: shades of green
with sheer in between create the striped pattern
on this unusual ribbon; satin ribbon printed with
multicoloured flowers; purple rickrack; hot pink
sheer ribbon with printed white spots.

# FLOWER-POWERED SUCCESS

Hark back to the hippy era and the heyday of flower power with this wacky car card in the shape of the beloved Bug (Beetle) – a unique way to congratulate someone on passing their driving test. The embossed areas and edges of the car are defined with blue chalk and then the body punctuated with different-sized daisies, punched from blue shimmer card. Blue crystals and iridescent glitter glue bring an extra glint to the flower centres as well as the embossed areas.

## YOU WILL NEED

❀ relief-embossed car-shaped folded card
❀ blue shimmer card
❀ blue chalk
❀ blue crystals
❀ iridescent glitter glue
❀ daisy punches – tiny, small and medium
❀ Basic Tool Kit (see page 110)

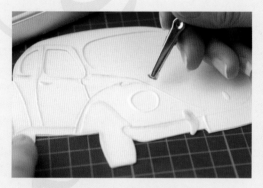

**1** Colour the embossed areas of the car-shaped card with blue chalk. Edge the windows and card with the same blue chalk.

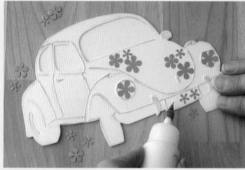

**2** Punch tiny, small and medium daisies from the blue shimmer card. Glue in groups over the car, using two medium daisies for the headlights and a row of three tiny daisies to denote the front number plate.

## Floral Focus

Try changing the colours of the punched flowers to orange and purple, and chalking the car in pink, or use flower peel-off stickers instead – the sparkly, almost holographic variety would be especially fun to use.

**3** Attach blue crystals to the centres of all the medium and small daisies. Add glitter glue to the centres of the tiny daisies, then edge the card and highlight the embossed areas with the glitter glue. Leave to dry.

# COMING OF AGE CARNIVAL

Give the signal that it's party time in no uncertain terms with this literally no-holes-barred see-through card design and let the good times roll! The flowers are die-cut in a selection of sizes from brightly coloured pearlescent card, with added punched centres embellished with glitter glue, as is the number '18', die-cut using the same system and cartridge. The concertina-folded card spine is punched with a series of double holes and each threaded with a different patterned ribbon in coordinating colours for a dazzling display.

## Floral Focus

The cutout style of the petals of these die-cut flowers is the ideal choice for this acetate card because they exploit the transparent quality of the medium and keep everything suitably see-through.

## Floral Bangle Tag

You can create this gift tag in no time at all, using some of the same die-cut flowers as for the card, to accompany a special present for the birthday girl or attached to the front of a plain card for another occasion. A simple white scallop-top tag has been edged with an orange inkpad and decorated with a wide band of orange and pink floral paper layered over a slightly wider band of the cherry card. The die-cut flowers are grouped and glued together as before, then attached to the tag and the hole threaded with spotted orange ribbon.

## CREATIVE CHOICES

❀ As the acetate is a neutral element, I was able to go wild here and choose a really vibrant combination of colours that will appeal to a young, trendy adult. As an equally appealing alternative, you could opt for turquoise and purple.

❀ The series of ribbon bows for the spine in a riot of designs adds a seriously funky note, but jewelled brads could be inserted instead, before you add the inside panel of card to conceal the double-sided tape used to attach the acetate.

## YOU WILL NEED

❀ acetate folded card, 14.8cm (6in) square

❀ pink textured card

❀ pearlescent card – pink, orange and cherry

❀ glitter glue – bright pink, pink and orange

❀ narrow ribbon – assorted patterns in pinks and oranges

❀ Cricut die-cutting system and George cartridge

❀ circle punches – small, medium and large

❀ Basic Tool Kit (see page 110)

1 Cut the acetate card in half to give you a separate front and back. Cut a strip of pink textured card 14.8 x 10cm (6 x 4in). Score down the length of the card three times, 2.5cm (1in) apart. Fold up concertina-style, then attach the outside edges to the acetate front and back using double-sided tape. Cut strips of the pink card 14.8 x 2.3cm (6 x ⅞in) and use to cover the double-sided tape.

2 Using the Cricut die-cutting system and George cartridge, die-cut a selection of different-sized flowers with cutout petals from the different-coloured pearlescent card.

**3** Using the small, medium and large circle punches, punch different-sized circles from the pearlescent card. Glue in place in the centres of the die-cut flowers, mixing and matching with the colours of the flowers.

**4** Cover the flower centres with glitter glue, using the colour to match the colour of the card. Leave to dry.

**5** Using the Cricut die-cutting system and George cartridge, die-cut a number '18' from pink pearlescent card. Die-cut a solid flower from orange card and a flower with cutout petals from cherry card, then glue the latter over the former. Layer the finished flower inside the card to make it easier to position the number '18' on the front of the card. Attach the number '18' to the card with double-sided tape. Place double-sided tape behind the number on the inside front of the card, then attach the flower, concealing the tape used to attach the number.

**6** Glue the flowers together by overlapping the petals, mixing the different sizes and colours. Glue to the concertina insert inside the card.

You could add a stamped message to the centre of the large flower, or stamp a message onto card, die-cut a circle around it using the same die-cutting system and attach it with the flowers or to the back of the card.

**7** Using a Japanese screw punch, punch a series of two holes, close together side by side, at evenly spaced intervals down the front spine of the card. Thread each set of holes with a different ribbon, tie in a knot and trim to equal length. Decorate the number '18' with pink glitter glue and leave to dry.

# MOTHER'S DAY DISPLAY

A gift of fresh flowers is the customary way of saying Happy Mother's Day, but here's an unexpected take on tradition that will give a lasting blast of colour and pleasure. Big, bold and bright die-cut blooms combined with smaller flowers are enhanced by a dotty relief pattern and contrasting punched centres, hole-punched and tied with vibrant ribbon for the large flowers and covered with dimensional fluid for the others. They are all attached to fluorescent-coloured looped drinking straws tied with more, acid-coloured ribbon, then displayed in a glass vase wrapped with ribbon and tied in a flamboyant bow.

## Floral Focus

By applying dots of dimensional fluid, the large daisy petals are given an interesting surface patterning, which echoes the relief-embossed pattern of little circles used to enhance the smaller daisies. Curling the petals adds further dimensional interest.

## Geometric Greeting

This easy yet zany card could accompany your Mother's Day display, but would also be perfect for a young girl's birthday. A large, square card is decorated inside with a spotted paper on one side and striped on the other, then the front folded back to form a 'Z'. A scallop-edged oblong is attached, overlapping, to the front and embellished with die-cut daisies patterned with dimensional fluid and embossing. A punched scallop-edged circle topped with a daisy is then half-glued to the card inside back so that it catches the oblong underneath to close.

## CREATIVE CHOICES

❀ I have used a whole mix of fun, vibrant colours and bold, graphic forms to deliberately get as far away from a naturalistic effect as possible, to maximize the funky impact.

❀ The sheer spotted ribbon wrapped around the vase and tied in a bow nicely reflects the textural patterning of the flower petals.

## YOU WILL NEED

❀ glass vase and coloured marbles

❀ die-cut card daisies – large and medium

❀ card in contrasting colours to the die-cut daisies

❀ ribbon in colours to match/coordinate with the daisies; patterned and sheer in coordinating colours; spotted green sheer wide

❀ coloured looped drinking straws

❀ dimensional fluid

❀ circle punches – medium and small

❀ die-cutting system and circles embossing folder

❀ Basic Tool Kit (see page 110)

**1** Apply dots of dimensional fluid all over the petals of the large die-cut daisies, but avoid adding any to the flower centres. Leave to dry for about 15–20 minutes.

**2** Using the medium circle punch, punch circles from contrasting-coloured card for the centres of the large daisies. Using a Japanese screw punch, punch two holes in the centre of each circle. Thread each flower centre with a length of ribbon in a colour to match or coordinate with the daisy petals but to contrast with the flower centre and tie in a knot. Trim the ends to an even length at an angle.

**3** Place each medium daisy in turn into the embossing folder, insert into the die-cutting system and press down to emboss the circles pattern onto the flower.

**4** Stretch each petal in turn around a smooth, round object, such as an embossing tool or a pen, to curl. Using the small circle punch, punch circles from contrasting-coloured card for the centres of the medium daisies and glue in place. Apply a coat of dimensional fluid all over each centre and leave to dry for about 15–20 minutes.

**5** Attach a drinking straw in a contrasting colour to the back of one petal of each large daisy using double-sided tape. Using the medium circle punch, punch a circle from card to match the colour of the petals of each flower and glue to the back of the petals, to cover the end of the straw.

**6** Tie a length of the patterned or sheer ribbon to each of the 'stems' on one side of the loops. Glue an embossed daisy on the opposite side of the loop and leave to dry.

Turn the vase upside down and tie the ribbon bow by creating two loops and tying together in a knot – this will ensure that the loops are at the top and the tails of the ribbon will hang down at the bottom.

**7** Wrap the spotted green sheer ribbon around the vase and tie in a bow to finish. Put glass marbles in the base of the vase before arranging the flowers to hold the stems in position.

# FOREVER SWEET 16

Celebrate a 16th birthday in a special way by creating a keepsake as a lasting reminder of the landmark event – you could also incorporate some photos to personalize it. Squares of patterned black and white papers are given a fancy stitched edging, then variously embellished and set against a vibrant orange painted canvas for maximum impact. Chipboard numbers are heat embossed to an alluringly glossy finish and then further enhanced with a stamped and embossed flower motif. Paper flowers with thread-tied button centres pretty up the picture. This versatile design would work equally well as an album cover or a scrapbook page.

## Floral Focus

Ready-made paper flowers are a quick and simple way to create this look. Alternatively, punch or die-cut your own from coloured card, printed papers or fabric – even coordinated with the birthday girl's bedroom décor.

## Paisley Patchwork

This stunning design also translates perfectly to a card. The squares of patterned papers are decorated in the same way but mounted onto an orange card, with the button-enhanced blooms punctuating the plainer panels. Spotted knotted ribbon tops it off in smart style.

## CREATIVE CHOICES

❀ The black and white background colour scheme I've chosen will work wonderfully with other strong colours – go as funky as you like with hot pink, lime green, purple or red.

❀ I opted for a symmetrical grid system for the underlying design, but a pleasing combination of oblongs and squares or a patchwork of smaller squares would be just as effective.

## YOU WILL NEED

❀ canvas, 30cm (12in) square

❀ orange acrylic paint

❀ black and white patterned papers – spotted, swirly and paisley

❀ ribbon – orange grosgrain, satin printed and narrow

❀ orange sewing thread

❀ topaz crystals

❀ orange glitter glue

❀ orange brads

❀ orange paper flowers

❀ orange buttons

❀ orange embroidery thread

❀ chipboard numbers '1' and '6'

❀ embossing inkpad

❀ ultra-thick embossing powder – orange and gold

❀ flower stamp

❀ round metal tag

❀ heat gun

❀ Basic Tool Kit (see page 110)

**1** Apply a coat of orange acrylic paint to the front of the canvas, working across the canvas, then leave to dry. Paint the edges and back of the canvas, ensuring that it is completely covered, then leave to dry. Apply a second coat to the front and edges, this time working down the canvas, until evenly covered, then leave to dry.

**2** Cut nine 9cm (3½in) squares from the patterned papers, three from each design. Cut four lengths of grosgrain ribbon and four of satin printed ribbon slightly longer/wider than the paper squares. Tie pairs of ribbon lengths together to create four knotted lengths, then attach to two spotted, one swirly and one paisley paper square with double-sided tape, trimming the excess ribbon. Using the orange sewing thread, machine stitch a row of zigzag stitches around the edges of all the squares.

When attaching the ribbon to the paper squares with double-sided tape, ensure that the tape goes over the edge of the paper, so that when the ribbon excess is trimmed, it will stop it from fraying.

**3** Now decorate the ribbonless squares. Fill the centres of the flowers on one of the swirly squares with crystals. Highlight details on one of the paisley squares with glitter glue, then leave to dry.

**4** On the second swirly square, cut a slit in the centre of each flower and insert a brad. Turn the paper over and open the brad 'wings' out flat on the reverse. On the remaining swirly square, add crystals to the flower centres and highlight details with the glitter glue.

**5** Glue tiny buttons to the centres of the small paper flowers. Decorate larger buttons with embroidery thread: starting at the front of the button, insert the thread through one hole to the back, then thread back through the other hole to the front. Repeat once more, then tie the thread in a double knot at the front and trim the excess.

**6** Paint the chipboard numbers with the orange paint. Ink the numbers with the embossing inkpad, then sprinkle with the orange embossing powder. Tap off the excess, then heat the powder with a heat gun to melt. Build up about three layers, until smooth and glass-like. Add highlights by heating areas and adding pinches of gold embossing powder. Ink the flower stamp with the embossing inkpad, heat an area on one of the numbers and stamp the motif into the molten embossing. Leave for a few seconds to cool before removing the stamp. Repeat several more times over both numbers. Apply glitter glue to the stamped petals.

**7** Attach double-sided tape to the reverse of each paper square, around the edges and across the centre. Adhere to the canvas in the arrangement shown in the photo on the opposite page, leaving an even gap between each square and the edges of the canvas. Attach the embossed numbers and flowers with foam pads. Glue a small flower with a threaded-button centre and a narrow ribbon bow to the metal tag, then mount onto the numbers with foam pads.

# BLOSSOMING IDEAS

No occasion would fail to benefit from the funky-flower treatment, and here are two classic events – a cause for congratulations and Christmas – that are given a design makeover to create some innovative items.

## WINNING FRAME

This intriguing design for a fresh-look congratulations card features an acetate frame with a floral design in relief, which has been embossed by placing in an embossing folder and running through a die-cutting system, then coloured in on the reverse with green and pink specialist pens. The translucent frame is then cleverly mounted onto the green panel, layered over the folded square pink card, by punching sets of double holes and threading with pink satin ribbon ties. Clusters of pink crystals add lustre to the flower centres of the embossed design.

**CREATIVE CHOICE**
I chose an embossing that allowed me to colour in the design on the reverse. Several other types of floral design would work, but you will need to assess first what areas they offer for colouring in.

**BEAUTIFUL OUTSIDE**
The same floral design is used to create a relief border for the envelope, this time embossed, using the same method as for the front frame, onto a strip of green card. Again, specialist pens are used to colour in the embossed elements of the design, pink for the flowers and green for the curly tendrils.

Using ribbon to attach the acetate frame to the card avoids you having to hide any glue or double-sided tape, and also adds to the appeal of the design.

# CHRISTMAS CANDLES

Light up someone's festive season with this striking design, featuring a cutout candle-shaped card. The flames are coloured using yellow, apricot and orange chalks and given added glow with glitter glue, while the candles are stamped all over with a gold funky flower shape, again highlighted with glitter glue for extra sparkle and edged top and bottom with green ribbon attached with double-sided tape. The punched poinsettias with small holes punched in the centre are backed with gold card and then layered offset over a second flower to produce double blooms. Die-cut baubles are 'hung' from lengths of rickrack braid and embellished with smaller poinsettias, again punched with holes so that the gold of the baubles shines through.

### CREATIVE CHOICE
I have chosen favourite Christmas motifs of poinsettia flowers and baubles, and used traditional festive colours of red, green and gold, but I've combined the elements in a bold, unconventional way to create an offbeat, funky feel.

### BEAUTIFULLY DIFFERENT
A single candle shape makes an ideal motif for an impressively tall card, in this case in seasonal gold, to create a quick and easy alternative design. It's decorated in just the same way as the multi-candle card, with just one die-cut bauble to match the gold card and a large, gold-backed poinsettia.

Be careful where you position the poinsettia flowers and baubles to ensure that you can still concertina-fold the card up, wrap with ribbon and place in an envelope.

# TRUE ROMANCE

# GET THE LOOK

To get into the mood of True Romance, go for those classic colours of love – luscious reds combined with glowing golds, sumptuous pinks, cool wedding whites and dreamy rich creams. Choose shimmer or pearlescent papers and card to up the element of glamour. While roses will always instantly say romance, I also love to use other flouncy blooms such as peonies or hydrangeas, which can be just as seductive. You can also make heart-shaped petals from rubber stamps, punches or even chipboard to create stunning blooms of your own. But don't stop there! Feel free to indulge in other sensuous embellishments such as gorgeous ribbons and sparkling gems, then personalize your wonderful creations with the couples' initials.

**This unusual floral paper** has a wonderfully romantic feel to it with its deep tones of rich red and deep, dark chocolate brown, and is sure to bring some passion to your projects. It reminds me of red roses and chocolates – the perfect combination for romance!

**Printed with many hearts** made of hugs and kisses, 'X's and 'O's, for a playful touch, this paper is also perfect for getting the romantic message across.

**Hearts and flowers** are scattered over the wavy coloured bands of this paper, which is sure to add a dynamic dimension to a design. It also offers plenty of scope for cutting out the different elements and using creatively in various ways.

**This stylized floral paper** while stylishly restrained in colour has a lively pattern that seems to dance in front of your eyes. It would be ideal for enhancing with glitter glue, crystals or flower sequins.

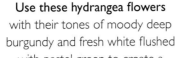

**Use these hydrangea flowers**
with their tones of moody deep
burgundy and fresh white flushed
with pastel green to create a
luxurious, opulent effect.

**These handmade quilled flowers**
are decadently frilly. This technique involves
cutting thin strips of paper to fringe them
and coiling the fringed strips with a quilling
tool. The glued coils are then opened up to
reveal the fabulous flowers. You can alter the
width of the paper strips to create larger or
smaller blooms.

**Generously petalled blooms**
in deep red, dramatic black and
milky white definitely have passion
power and will give a striking look
to your cards.

**These white plasma flowers**
have a slightly frosted appearance for a
cool, sophisticated effect. Try stamping
on them with permanent inkpads or
colouring the edges. They can also be
embellished with crystals, brads and
ribbon in suitably romantic hues.

**Buttons in red and pale pink**
make ideal embellishments for True
Romance papercrafted items, especially
in groups of different sizes. Use as they
are or tie thread, string or narrow
ribbon to their centres.

**These heart-shaped brads**
in all tones of pink are guaranteed to
give your cards the look of love!

**Use these distinctive ribbons and braid**
to reinforce the romantic feel: deep red velvet
rickrack, for added texture; cream sheer ribbon
with a pattern of swirly scrolls – ideal for wedding
designs; pink grosgrain ribbon with printed flowers;
cream sheer ribbon with white spots.

# WEDDING LACE WINDOW

Mark the happy occasion in memorably good taste with this de luxe design of understated elegance. Daisies of different sizes are punched from the same cream-coloured cardstock as the base card and glued together to create a lace-like panel in an offset window cut in the front, the linen texture of the card enhancing the fabric feel. Iridescent crystals and glitter glue add subtle yet opulent highlights.

## YOU WILL NEED

✤ cream linen-textured folded card, 14.8cm (6in) square, plus extra for punching

✤ AB crystals

✤ iridescent glitter glue

✤ jumbo square punch

✤ daisy punch – tiny, small and medium

✤ Basic Tool Kit (see page 110)

**1** To create the rectangular aperture, open the folded card out and lay right-side up on a cutting mat. Position the square punch along the top of the card on the right-hand side and punch out a square. Align the punch with the bottom of the card and punch out a second square.

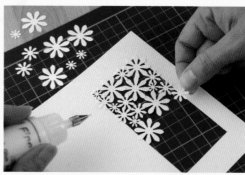

**2** Punch flowers in an assortment of sizes from the extra card. Starting at the top of the aperture, glue the edges of the flower petals to the card and then to other overlapping petal edges. Continue working down the card until the aperture is completely filled.

## Floral Focus

Try using other types of flower for this lacy look – a stylized, Mary Quant-style flower, for instance, would bring a very different, retro quality to the design.

**3** Glue crystals to the centres of the medium and large flowers. Fill the centres of the smallest flowers with glitter glue. Leave to dry.

# LOVE-PETALS FOR LONGING

Are you wishing they were here? If so, why not communicate those longing feelings for the love in your life in a creative way. This card conveys the message in style, with a subtle design in soft tones of cream and pale pink. The focal embellishment for the grid of square apertures is a single bloom formed from stamped floral-patterned heart-shaped petals, curled to give dimensional interest and enriched with glitter glue highlights. Knotted lengths of pale pink ribbon and trios of crystals add the final decorative touches.

## Floral Focus

The stamped heart-shaped petals of the central flower reflect the romantic theme in a sophisticated, subtle way. Instead of a single flower, create a bouquet of three flowers with different sized and shaped stamped hearts, then attach green ribbon stems and mount onto a plain card without an aperture, wrapped with floral-patterned paper.

## Singular Sentiment

This plain pink, tall card features a single flower with heart-shaped petals in proportions to match, atop an elegant long stem of pink grosgrain ribbon. Onto this I have threaded a narrow tag, stamped with a simple pink flower head and a crystal added to the centre to echo the main flower, then edged with pink ink and iridescent glitter glue. A second length of the ribbon is tied to the stem to form stylized leaves. This would make a lovely sympathy or thinking of you card.

## CREATIVE CHOICES

❀ The colours I have chosen here are soft and sensuous, in keeping with the romantic mood, but for a more unconventional approach, why not try rich golds or coppers and warm oranges for stamping the flowers and for the ribbon and crystals.

❀ The pink grosgrain ribbon is a classic choice for this theme, but you could use sheer organdie ribbon for a more delicate, luxurious effect, or use patterned ribbon teamed with a plain stamped heart for the flower petals.

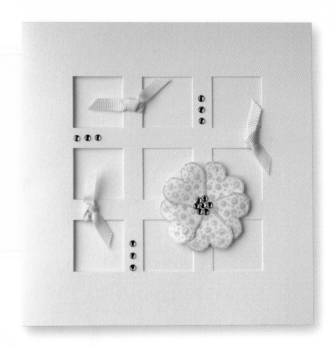

## YOU WILL NEED

❀ gold shimmer card

❀ gold shimmer nine-square aperture folded card, 14.8cm (6in) square

❀ floral-patterned heart stamp and acrylic block

❀ rose pink inkpad

❀ iridescent glitter glue

❀ soft pink crystals

❀ pink narrow grosgrain ribbon

❀ Basic Tool Kit (see page 110)

**1** Using the acrylic block, stamp the floral heart design in rose pink ink onto the gold shimmer card. Repeat until you have five prints in total.

Place a small stamp at one corner of the acrylic block before placing the stamp to be used on the block, then ink up, avoiding the small stamp, and print the design – the small stamp helps to balance the block and prevent you from rocking and spoiling the image.

**2** Cut out the five stamped hearts. Stretch the two lobes of each heart over a smooth, round object, such as an embossing tool or a pen, to curl and give petal-like dimension to the shapes.

**3** Highlight the stamped floral pattern on the heart petals and the edge of each heart petal with iridescent glitter glue. Leave to dry thoroughly.

**4** To stick the five heart petals together to form a single flower, apply glue to the bottom point of one petal, then add the next petal on top.

**5** Glue a group of the crystals to the centre of the flower, then mount the flower onto the folded card between the apertures using foam pads.

**6** Cut three lengths of the pink ribbon. Tie each in a double knot around a border between apertures, positioned to the left, above and right of the flower. Trim the ends of the ribbon to an even length at an angle.

A perfect positioner, consisting of a stick with a lump of wax on the end used by beaders, is the ideal tool for picking up crystals. Have the crystal the right way up, touch down with the perfect positioner to pick the crystal up, then place on the glue and let go.

**7** Glue a row of three crystals to the remaining borders between the apertures.

# INVITING ROSES

Set the scene for a celebratory event filled with the sweet scent of romance with these rose-adorned engagement party invitations. The ribbon-tied front panels, embellished with a heart-shaped wreath of stamped and cutout rose heads and personalized with the betrothed's initials, open to reveal the whole stamped rose stems framed within a die-cut cream card circle edged with a pink scalloped border. A second, shaped layer of rose heads gives the design added depth and prominence. This central flap lifts to uncover a pink scalloped-edged pocket, again decorated with stamped rose heads, which holds another die-cut card circle, this time for framing the details of the occasion.

## Floral Focus

The stamped rose design I have used here is very much contemporary in design, but for a different look or to suit the style of the occasion, choose one that has a more traditional appeal.

## Beautiful Bouquet

If time is in short supply, make this simpler yet sumptuous variation on the same theme for the invites, or use as an engagement card. The central rose bouquet design is stamped onto a white card panel, then mounted onto a scallop-edged rectangle of red card to create a distinctive, ruffle-style frame. The red ribbon tie adds a textural flourish.

## CREATIVE CHOICES

❀ I chose a palette of soft cream and pastel pinks, with a touch of lime green, for a light, fresh look, but for a more formal, richer effect, opt for deep red and gold, and use plain-coloured pearlized papers for stamping onto rather than patterned papers.

❀ The composition of the design on the inside scallop-edged pocket of the invite allows enough space to add the date of the wedding above the row of rose heads – you could use a computer to print it out in a fancy font.

## YOU WILL NEED

❀ patterned papers
 – pink floral and green

❀ double-fold cream card with central inside flap, 14.8cm (6in) square

❀ cream card

❀ pink scallop-edged card, 7.5 x 12.4cm (3 x 5in)

❀ roses stamp

❀ black inkpad

❀ pink crystals

❀ iridescent glitter glue

❀ mini chipboard letters

❀ pink sheer narrow ribbon

❀ die-cutting system and circle and scallop-edged circle dies

❀ 2 pink eyelets and eyelet-setting tools

❀ Basic Tool Kit
 (see page 110)

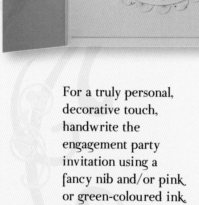

For a truly personal, decorative touch, handwrite the engagement party invitation using a fancy nib and/or pink or green-coloured ink.

**1** Using the black inkpad, stamp just a single rose head a total of 18 times onto the pink floral-patterned paper and leave to dry. Cut out each rose head.

**2** Trace around the heart template on page 116 and cut out. Lay on the centre front of the closed-up double-fold cream card. Make a series of evenly spaced pencil marks around the heart as a guide to positioning the rose heads, then glue cutout rose heads in place to form a complete heart. Add a crystal below each rose head and decorate the centres with glitter glue, then leave to dry.

**3** Apply glue to the front of each chipboard letter, top with a piece of the pink floral-patterned paper and smooth down. Leave to dry for about 10 minutes. Turn each letter over and trim around it with a craft knife. Glue one letter to each front panel of the card within the heart. Edge the letters with the glitter glue and leave to dry.

**4** Stamp the whole roses design onto cream card and leave to dry. Using the die-cutting system, align the circle die with the stamped design, secure in place with tape and die-cut the stamped circle. Using the die-cutting system, die-cut a scallop-edged circle from the pink floral-patterned paper. Glue the stamped circle to the scallop-edged circle and mount onto the central inside flap.

**5** Stamp the rose design twice onto the pink patterned paper and once onto the green patterned paper. Cut out all the leaves from the green paper and glue in place on the stamped design on the cream circle. Cut out one set of rose heads from the pink paper and glue in place. Cut out the remaining set of rose heads, then stretch over a smooth, round object, such as an embossing tool or a pen, to curl. Layer over the first rose heads.

**6** Stamp just a single rose head eight times onto the pink floral-patterned paper and leave to dry. Cut out and glue seven in a horizontal row along the centre of the scallop-edged rectangle of pink card. Attach double-sided tape to the back of the pink card along the sides and bottom edge and attach to the central inside panel of the card (beneath the flap) to create a pocket. Glue a crystal below each rose head and decorate the centres with glitter glue.

**7** For the invite itself, die-cut a circle from the cream card and a scallop-edged circle from the pink floral-patterned paper, as in Step 4. Glue the cream card circle to the scallop-edged circle. Add the remaining rose head to the top centre, with a crystal below. Tuck into the scallop-edged pocket. Set a pink eyelet either side of the front opening of the card, thread with ribbon and tie to close.

# EMBOSSED WEDDING BOOK

Say a special thank you to the bride and groom's parents or bridesmaids with this personalized wedding book in celebration of the great event. The covers of this lavish little tome, featuring the initials of the happy couple, untie to reveal an accordion of pages elegantly adorned with red and gold flowers and a glitter-edged heart, striped paper borders and glitter glue-enhanced wedding date. It incorporates two frames for displaying photos of the wedding party, ready-embossed with a pretty paisley design that is coloured with chalks and highlighted with glitter glue, and further embellished with ribbon and glitter-centred flowers.

## Floral Focus

The embossed paisley design of the decorative frames is brought to life by colouring in the background with a warm-coloured chalk, then picking out the leaves in pastel pink chalk and highlighting the dainty flowers with touches of spangly red glitter glue.

## Perfectly Framed

This simpler version still offers the capacity to capture two special moments from the big day. The inside is easily created by scoring a long rectangle of card twice down the centre to create a gusset, then attaching an embossed frame either side with foam pads. The pretty relief flower design has again been enhanced with chalks and glitter glue, and the printed pattern on the covers also highlighted with glitter glue and embellished by a band of contrasting paper. A deep pink flower punctuates the glitter-covered, painted initials.

## CREATIVE CHOICES

❀ To create a suitably sumptuous effect, I have chosen a rich and romantic colour scheme of pink, soft red and gold, with touches of deep red for added drama and glitter glue highlights for extra glitz. Alternatively, you could choose colours to coordinate with the wedding scheme.

❀ I picked the paisley design for the embossed frames because the leaves form a subtle, sinuous pattern, which adds interest but doesn't threaten to overwhelm the other decorative elements, or indeed the photos, especially coloured with soft chalks.

## YOU WILL NEED

❀ 2 chipboard squares, 12.5cm (5in), letters and mini numbers

❀ patterned papers – pink and yellow floral, soft red and pink striped

❀ cream accordion card, 12.5cm (5in) square

❀ pearlescent gold paper

❀ glitter glue – platinum and red

❀ ribbon – soft brown/beige and red narrow

❀ gold inkpad

❀ 2 paisley embossed frames

❀ chalks – golden brown and pale pink

❀ gold-coloured paint

❀ petals/hearts template

❀ small circle punch

❀ Basic Tool Kit (see page 110)

**1** Cut two pieces of the pink and yellow floral-patterned paper to cover one side of the chipboard squares, allowing an extra 2cm (¾in) all the way around to glue to the back of the chipboard. Cover the chipboard squares with glue, lay the patterned paper on top and smooth down. Trim the corners at an angle, fold the excess over to the back of the chipboard square and attach with double-sided tape.

**2** Apply glue to the front of the chipboard letters, cover with the soft red patterned paper and smooth down. Leave to dry for 10 minutes. Turn over and trim with a craft knife. Edge the letters with platinum glitter glue and leave to dry. Tie a length of soft brown/beige and a length of red ribbon around each letter.

**3** Colour around the edges of the pages of the accordion card using a gold inkpad. Attach a length of red ribbon at right angles to the outside edge of each chipboard cover on the back, then attach the covers to the accordion card using double-sided tape.

**4** Colour the background of the embossed frames around the paisley motifs with golden brown chalk, then use pale pink chalk to fill in the paisley design, adding the flower detail in red glitter glue. Attach the frames to the first and third pages of the accordion book using foam pads around the sides and bottom only, to allow photos to be inserted. Wrap one frame with red ribbon and tie to secure.

**5** Cover the chipboard numbers with gold-coloured paint and leave to dry. Cover the numbers with platinum glitter glue and leave to dry. Cut a strip of the pink striped paper and attach horizontally to the second page of the accordion book. Mount the numbers in a row above using foam pads.

**6** Draw around three different petal shapes of the template onto the gold and soft red patterned paper, folded concertina-style, and cut out. Using the small circle punch, punch circles from the gold and red paper. Glue the petals to the back of contrasting-coloured punched circles. Stretch each petal around a smooth, round object, such as an embossing tool or a pen, to curl. Edge the petals and fill the flower centres with platinum glitter glue, or red glitter glue for the red centres. Leave to dry.

**7** Trace around the larger heart on the template onto the gold paper and cut out. Attach to the last page of the accordion book. Add strips of the pink striped paper overlapping the heart. Cut out a smaller heart from the gold paper and glue to the front cover, overlapping a short strip of the pink striped paper. Edge around the hearts with glitter glue and leave to dry. Add the flowers to the front cover and accordion pages.

Folding the paper concertina-style before drawing around the petal shapes not only gives you several in one go but ensures that they match in size and shape.

# BLOSSOMING IDEAS

The romantic treatment can be applied to all sorts of occasions beyond the obvious events such as Valentine's Day and wedding anniversaries, as these designs show. It's all about a sensuous use of both colour and texture to communicate a feeling of warmth and love.

## HOME SWEET HOME

Give a loving couple a warm welcome to their new nest with this pretty-as-a-picture house. Card windows and a door, inked around the edges to stand out, are glued to the shaped card, which is edged around the sides and bottom in the same way. Diamond-patterned paper is attached to the roof, with the bottom row of diamonds cut out and curled up to add dimension. Window boxes and planters adorn the facade, filled with flowers colour coordinated with the roof, and punched flowers form a smoke-like trail rising from the chimney. You could personalize the card by adding the appropriate house number.

### CREATIVE CHOICES
Choosing a house-shaped card gets the message across instantly, while using the diamond-patterned paper is a quick and colourful way of suggesting roof tiles.

**BEAUTIFUL OUTSIDE**
For a stylish matching envelope, a wide border of the same patterned paper as used for the house-card roof is glued to the left-hand side of the envelope front, then overlapped with a punched scallop-edged oval address label, which has been edged with ink in the same way as the card.

# NUMBER 1 GIRL

Celebrate your favourite baby girl's first birthday with this dazzling design in pinks and white. Flowers are stamped all over the scallop-shaped tag card and a pink plasma number '1' using a white inkpad. The number is then traced around on the back of white card and cut out, leaving a narrow border of card, and two holes punched in the centre of both card and plasma numbers, through which spotted ribbon is threaded and tied. Silver glitter gel pen is used to highlight the card and number edges, and pink glitter glue for adding light-catching centres to the flowers. The number is mounted with foam pads.

Add a photograph of the baby girl or the baby's name to the card to give it a personalized dimension.

### CREATIVE CHOICE
Change the deep pink and white colour scheme to a bright turquoise blue, use stars instead of flowers and finish with a bold striped ribbon to transform the design into a baby boy's first birthday card.

**BEAUTIFUL INSIDE**
The same stamped flower motif is used to decorate the inside of the tag card, but this time stamped three times onto pink card and punched out using a circle punch upside down as a guide to positioning. The circles are edged with the glitter gel pen and mounted onto the card with foam pads, then glitter glue centres added.

# VINTAGE VOGUE

# GET THE LOOK

To achieve the Vintage Vogue look, I've chosen muted yet warm tones for the patterned papers and colour schemes, such as olive greens, browns, ivory and deep reds. I've also given the projects a textural richness, using textured card, velvet ribbons and fabric flowers. Subtle and stylized retro floral patterns give the right vintage feel, with layered double blooms and frilly-petalled flowers adding an element of old-style opulence. Create your own elegant floral embellishments by cutting out petals from pearlized papers using a template and assembling them into beautiful blooms. Edges of petals as well as card can be coloured with brown ink to enhance the aged effect, and glitter-coated brads, thread-tied buttons and crystal gems used to add sparkle and interest to flower centres.

**This classy printed paper** sprinkled with tiny flowers is a lovely subtle shade of olive green – perfect for a period feel. A bright green just would not work for this theme.

**This deep red paper** also has a soft, subdued style of pattern, printed all over with paler red heart-shaped flowers, for that essential vintage quality. It would look stunning with some dainty lace embellishments.

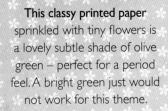

**Delicately patterned,** this paper again has just the right laid-back colours for the Vintage Vogue look. The deep red flowers would look fabulous with pearls added to their centres.

**Velvet-flocked flowers** are the distinctive feature of this stylized patterned paper, making it a must for a Vintage Vogue project.

**These hydrangea flowers**
are simply irresistible with their
wonderfully faded, dusky pink petals
and centres of the softest olive green.

**Rich velvet flowers**
will instantly add textural interest to
any papercrafted item. They make
you want to reach out and stroke
their lovely soft, plush petals.

**Tiny, deep brown metal brads**
have an appropriate aged feel to them.
In fact, they look like nail heads.

**Pretty pale paper flowers**
can be layered to create
luxurious double blooms or
used singly. These would look
particularly lovely with a pearl
button in each centre.

**These mother-of-pearl buttons**
in flower shapes would look highly
effective added to an olive green
patterned paper, threaded with pink
sheer narrow ribbon.

**This pewter-coloured sticker**
with a deeply etched floral design
layered onto a card and a brooch
pin added to the back would make a
card and gift in one.

**These handsome metal buckles**
have an open design detail that can be
enhanced to great effect by threading
with ribbon so that glimpses of it can
be seen through the apertures.

**These richly textured, retro ribbons** beautiful
reflect the vintage mood: wider-width brown
satin ribbon with a printed flower design;
luxurious deep green velvet rickrack; knocked-
back cream, pink, blue and brown woven floral-
patterned ribbon; soft pink velvet ribbon.

# FRIENDSHIP FRIEZE

True friendship is a precious commodity, so why not show your appreciation of someone's affection and support by re-creating this classically composed card incorporating an elegant flower brooch. In this subtle two-tone scheme, two flower stickers overlay a border sticker, each layered onto card and a brooch pin added to the small flower tile, together with glitter glue highlights. Mounted with foam pads, they are complemented by a row of blue crystals.

## YOU WILL NEED

❀ soft blue textured folded card, 14.8cm (6in) square
❀ soft blue textured card
❀ brown inkpad
❀ sheet of flower stickers
❀ brooch pin
❀ 3 blue crystals
❀ iridescent glitter glue
❀ Basic Tool Kit (see page 110)

**1** Ink the edges of the folded card with the brown inkpad. Lift the wiggly-edged flower border sticker from the sheet of stickers and attach vertically down the right-hand side of the card.

**2** Cut the single flower sticker and frame from the sheet and layer onto the soft blue textured card. Trim, leaving a narrow border of card all the way around. Ink the edges of the card to match the main card. Attach the brooch pin to the back of the flower tile.

## Floral Focus

The watercolour effect on these flower stickers gives their colours a soft, muted quality, which results in a fine-art feel.

**3** Layer the floral frieze sticker onto the same soft blue card and trim to the edge of the sticker. Mount onto the main card with foam pads. Attach foam pads either side of he brooch pin and mount onto the frieze sticker. Glue three crystals in a horizontal row below the sticker. Decorate the flower tile with glitter glue, then leave to dry.

# LACED WITH LOVE

Why not devote a little of your time to making a unique token of your love in the
form of a handcrafted Valentine's Day card, which your partner can then preserve
as a testament to those shared special moments. A bold, retro-style patterned
paper in dusky vintage tones is mounted onto a plain cream card, leaving only
a narrow border, and decorated with punched hearts. Overlaid is a cream
card band, given an antiqued look by inking the edges and laced together with
sumptuous old-world velvet ribbon. Full-blown punched pink blooms with inked
and curled petals and tied-thread button centres complete the sensuous effect.

## Floral Focus

These classy pink blooms are appropriately opulent
for the occasion, achieved by gluing together two
punched card flowers and shaping the petals.
Try die-cutting felt or fabric flowers instead, or
create them from velvet, which will give them a
wonderful textural dimension and bring an extra
luxurious quality to the card.

## Antique Pouch

This simple, any-occasion card offers the same retro appeal. Three-
quarters of the card is covered with the patterned paper, leaving the
top open for the tag, then the opening edged with a brown card strip
topped with pink velvet ribbon. The plain card and tag edges are inked
to enhance the aged effect, and the patterned paper added to the
tag bottom and a punched double bloom at the top, with a punched
brown card and button centre. A second bloom balances the design.

## CREATIVE CHOICES

❊ The classic Valentine's colour scheme of pink and red is used here, but the design would work equally well for a wedding anniversary made in warm oranges, browns and copper tones, with a sheer organdie ribbon for a soft, delicate touch.

❊ Punched pink pearlescent hearts glued to the patterned paper project the romantic theme, but small punched flowers in the same style as the large ones could be used instead to make a birthday or thank you card.

❊ In place of the stylized flower-patterned paper, choose a more traditional floral paper and add pearl buttons to reinforce the look.

## YOU WILL NEED

❊ red, pink and cream circle-patterned paper

❊ cream folded card, 14.8cm (6in) square

❊ cream card

❊ pink pearlescent card

❊ brown chalk inkpad

❊ pink narrow velvet ribbon

❊ 3 deep red buttons

❊ pink embroidery thread

❊ punches – corner rounder and medium daisy

❊ paddle punch and small heart die

❊ Basic Tool Kit (see page 110)

**1** Cut a 14.3cm (5¾in) square from the patterned paper. Ink the edges of the square with a brown chalk inkpad. Attach centrally to the cream folded card with double-sided tape.

**2** Cut two pieces of cream card 6 x 10cm (2½ x 4in) and 6 x 4cm (2½ x 1½in). Using the corner rounder punch, round the corners of one short edge of each piece. Ink the edges with the inkpad.

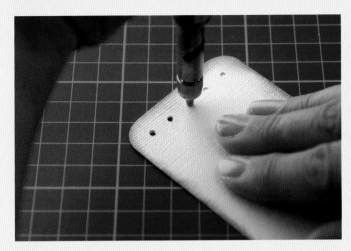

**3** Using a Japanese screw punch, punch five holes along the rounded short edge of one piece of cream card 1cm (⅜in) apart. Repeat with the other piece of cream card by placing the punched card on top and punching through the holes, so that they are exactly aligned.

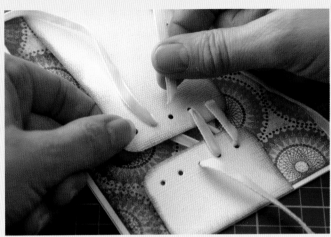

**4** Stick the unpunched edges of the card pieces to the sides of the card towards the bottom edge with double-sided tape. Trim one end of the length of ribbon to a point, then thread through the punched holes, starting from the top and threading from the front to the back, then cross over to the other side and thread from the back to the front. At the bottom, tie the ribbon in a double knot.

**5** Using the medium daisy punch, punch six daisies from pink pearlescent card and ink the edges with the brown chalk inkpad. Glue together in pairs to make double blooms. Stretch the petals over a smooth, round object, such as an embossing tool or a pen, to curl.

**6** Attach the flowers to the laced card with foam pads. Thread the buttons with the embroidery thread, tie in a knot and trim the ends. Glue to the flower centres.

If you have trouble threading the ribbon through the holes in the card, use a darning needle, which has a large eye, to thread it.

**7** Using the paddle punch and heart die, punch hearts from the pink pearlescent card. Glue to the circle centres on the patterned paper.

# WELCOME BASKET

There's something about a basket that's always reassuring and inviting, with its pleasing, homely form and promise of treats inside, so what could be more appropriate for a new home gift, filled with welcoming goodies. This one may look elaborate, but it's easily constructed from die-cut card circles covered with nostalgic, country-style patterned papers in warming tones, scored down the sides and bottom and taped together, then laced with pretty ribbon ties. Flouncy-petalled flowers hand-cut from pearlized papers add to the decorative effect, framing the focal embellishment of the house and heart motifs.

## Floral Focus

I chose these petals with pointed edges so that when combined together to make a whole flower head they create a strong, distinctive shape and stand out against the patterned background of the basket.

## Prettily Packaged

Use the same floral-patterned paper to giftwrap a luxury bar of chocolate for an always-welcome gift. The printed pattern is enhanced with teal-coloured glitter glue, as is a strip of doily-style paper, which is then glued across the package front. Apricot paper flowers, their centres studded with amber-coloured jewels, complete the vintage look. Transform a die-cut matt to wrap around the package to match, adding a second decorative paper strip tied in a knot, flattened and attached to the first, and a ribbon bow – fabulous as a wedding favour with the addition of the big event's date.

## CREATIVE CHOICES

❀ I chose these particular patterned papers because of their period-look brown and ivory tones, lifted with touches of teal, which are then 'aged' with a brown inkpad to achieve the desired vintage quality.

❀ Covering the basket sides in different yet coordinating patterned papers creates an appealing patchwork effect. This could be enhanced by adding hand-drawn stitch marks around the edges or even stamped or rub-on stitches.

## YOU WILL NEED

❀ brown, ivory and teal patterned papers

❀ 5 die-cut card circles, 12.8cm (5in) in diameter

❀ pearlescent papers – brown, ivory and teal

❀ pearlescent card – dark brown and beige

❀ brown inkpad

❀ ribbon – cream narrow; cream, beige and pale blue velvet in different, wider widths

❀ brown, teal and iridescent glitter glue

❀ scoreboard

❀ petals template

❀ punches – small circle and heart

❀ Basic Tool Kit (see page 110)

**1** Cut strips of the different patterned papers approximately 15 x 7.5cm (6 x 3in). Colour the edges using a brown inkpad. Glue the strips to the front of the die-cut circles, one complete strip on one side of each circle and two to cover the remaining part of each circle. Trim the excess paper. Colour the outside edges of the circles with the brown inkpad. Cover the reverse side of each circle with a single piece of patterned paper, the same design for each circle.

**2** Score three sides of the front of four of the circles using a scoreboard, leaving the fifth circle unscored for the base of the basket. Line up the edge of the circle against one scored line and score down the next one. Repeat for the remaining two sides.

**3** Using a Japanese screw punch, punch a row of evenly spaced holes down the scored areas of each circle. Fold the scored sides inwards. Place lengths of double-sided tape just outside the three scored sides of each circle and to the four sides of the unscored base circle and attach the circles together to form a basket shape. Thread a length of cream narrow ribbon through each set of holes and tie together, trimming the ends to an even length at an angle.

**4** Fold the brown, ivory and teal pearlescent papers concertina-style, then place the petal template on top, draw around and cut out. Cut out a variety of different-sized petals to make flowers of varying sizes.

**5** Using the small circle punch, punch circles for the centres of the flowers from the pearlescent papers. Cover with glue and place the petals, evenly spaced, onto the circles. Stretch each petal in turn over a smooth, round object, such as an embossing tool or a pen, to curl. Add matching-coloured glitter glue to the centres and leave to dry. Attach to the basket using foam pads.

**6** Cut a long, narrow strip of dark brown pearlescent card for the basket handle. Glue each end to either side of the basket on the inside. Tie lengths of cream, beige and pale blue ribbon in different widths to the handle on either side.

Once you have made the flowers but before curling the petals, edge them with iridescent glitter for an extra touch of sparkle and leave to dry – it is easier to apply the glitter glue to a flat surface.

**7** Using the template on page 117, cut out the house from dark brown pearlescent card. Using the heart punch, punch a heart from beige pearlescent card and glue to the centre of the house. Mount the house onto the front of the basket using foam pads.

# ANNIVERSARY ANNOUNCEMENT

The occasion of a first wedding anniversary is usually a more intimate event than the public proclamation of the big day itself, but no less worthy of acknowledgment. So give the happy couple the opportunity to record and display their personal celebrations in the form of photos and other precious mementos on this romantically styled notice board. It is simply constructed from chipboard covered with patterned paper, taped with a two-tone webbing of ribbon, the top layer of which is secured to the board by double fabric flowers with glitter-coated brad centres. Layered chipboard hearts in coordinating papers and tiny punched pink card hearts tied with ribbon, decorated with glitter glue and loose glitter respectively, enrich the embellishment.

## Floral Focus

Choose velvet fabric flowers for a rich, sumptuous effect and an instant old-fashioned feel. Whatever colour you favour, it will coordinate effortlessly with the appropriate floral-patterned paper.

## Heartfelt Greetings

This charming, quick-to-make card is the perfect accompaniment to the notice board anniversary gift. The same floral-patterned paper is attached to three-quarters of a folded card and bordered with a ribbon band, then topped with a chipboard heart covered in a contrasting paper from the same collection, edged with glitter glue. A single layered bloom is mounted with a foam pad over the top and balanced by three glitter-coated brads added to the bottom right-hand corner.

## CREATIVE CHOICES

❀ The turquoise provides a distinctive contrasting colour to the pink in this design, but be prepared to adapt the scheme so that the colours not only work with each other but in the context of the couples' home décor.

❀ Brads offer an easy way to hold the ribbon in place, and they are decorative too! This glitter-coated variety also adds an attractive sparkle.

## YOU WILL NEED

❀ sheet of chipboard, 30cm (12in) square

❀ pink and turquoise patterned paper in 2 coordinating designs

❀ pink card

❀ ribbon – pale pink wide and deep pink narrower grosgrain; pale pink narrow satin

❀ 13 small pink and 13 large turquoise fabric flowers

❀ pink and turquoise glitter-coated brads

❀ large and medium chipboard hearts

❀ deep pink glitter glue and loose glitter

❀ photo frame

❀ sticky sheet

❀ paddle punch and small heart die

❀ Basic Tool Kit (see page 110)

**1** Cut a 30cm (12in) square of one type of patterned paper. Apply thick craft glue to the front of the sheet of chipboard, place the patterned paper on top and smooth down. Leave to dry for about 10 minutes.

**2** Using double-sided tape, attach a length of the pale pink grosgrain ribbon to the covered chipboard from the top left-hand corner to the bottom right-hand corner. Repeat for the opposite diagonal. Mark the centre of each side, then attach lengths of ribbon from one mark on one side to the mark on the adjacent side to create grid lines.

**3** Layer a pink flower over each turquoise flower by pushing the 'wings' of a glitter-coated brad through the centre of the pink flower, then through the turquoise flower, but don't open the 'wings' out flat as yet.

**4** Cut lengths of the deep pink ribbon and position over the pale pink grid lines. Using a Japanese screw punch, punch a hole where the lengths of ribbon intersect through both layers of ribbon, the paper and chipboard. Thread the 'wings' of a brad in a flower centre through each hole to the back of the notice board, then open the 'wings' out flat at the back to secure. Secure the ends of the deep pink ribbon with double-sided tape and trim to size.

**5** Cut lengths of the deep pink ribbon for each side of the notice board. Attach lengths of double-side tape to the patterned paper along each side, ensuring that no flower petals are caught underneath. Lay a length of ribbon onto the tape, turn the ends over the board edges to the back and secure. Repeat for the remaining sides. Trim the petals of the flowers to the edge of the board – you may find this easier with the board back facing you. Cut a length of deep pink ribbon for hanging and attach to the back of the board at the top by securing with the brad 'wings'.

**6** Apply glue to the front of the large chipboard heart, top with the other type of patterned paper and smooth down, then leave to dry for 10 minutes. Repeat with the other chipboard heart and the first patterned paper. Turn the hearts over and trim around the edges with a craft knife. Edge each heart with the glitter glue and leave to dry. Adhere the medium heart to the centre of the large heart, using glue or double-sided tape, then tuck behind the deep pink ribbon webbing of the notice board to secure.

**7** Stick the pink card to the back of the sticky sheet. Using the paddle punch and die, cut three hearts from the card-backed sticky sheet. Remove the backing paper from each heart and sprinkle with loose glitter, tapping off the excess. Using a Japanese screw punch, punch a hole at the top of each heart, thread with pale pink narrow satin ribbon and tie to the deep pink ribbon on the board. Tie the photo frame to the board with ribbon in the same way. Cover the back of the notice board with patterned paper.

You can create your own glitter-coated brads by applying PVA (white) glue to the top of the brad, dipping into loose glitter and tapping off the excess. Leave to dry thoroughly before using.

# BLOSSOMING IDEAS

Here are two more ideas for greetings cards for other key occasions, which share the same enduringly traditional vintage appeal in their basic design as the other projects in this section.

## SOOTHING ASYMMETRY

The subtle and serene qualities of this card perfectly reflect its message of sincere sympathy. A strip of patterned paper is overlaid with a narrow decorative paper ribbon, positioned both off-centre on the card and in relation to each other. Two fabric flowers are layered on top, mounted with foam pads to create depth, and the centre decorated with crystals.

> ### CREATIVE CHOICE
> I have especially selected soft, subdued colours here to reinforce the feeling of comfort and contemplation.

### BEAUTIFUL INSIDE
The design for the inside picks up the two main elements from the front – the patterned paper, in a short wide strip, and a fabric flower with a crystal centre, mounted with a foam pad again off-centre and overhanging.

The daisy is pretty yet understated, perfect for this card. As the lily is a suitably symbolic flower for sympathy cards, you could use a silk lily bloom instead, which would also tone well with the muted colour scheme.

# BUGGY BLISS

Welcome the latest addition into the family fold with this lively, textural design. The background is a simple montage of four toning patterned paper squares, while the pram is quickly created by cutting a quarter from a card circle, with two smaller circles for wheels. The pram surface is covered with flower shapes punched from softly patterned pink paper, attached with glue, with two larger flowers to resemble wheel spokes. Light-catching crystals added to the flower centres draw the eye for a finishing flourish.

### CREATIVE CHOICE
The pastel pink tones unify the different, 'busy' elements of the design, but you could apply the same principle to a blue colour theme for a boy.

 Cover other instantly baby-associated shapes with punched flowers, such as a bib or teddy bear – and both are suitable for a boy or girl.

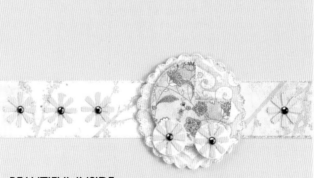

### BEAUTIFUL INSIDE
The same pram motif in miniature brings lift to the inside too, as it appears to trundle along a strip of patterned paper, mounted onto a scallop-edged circle with a foam pad. Punched pink card flowers with crystal centres again denote the wheels as well as decorate the strip.

# BASIC TOOL KIT

Each project in the book details any specialist tools and equipment required in the accompanying 'You Will Need' lists, but there are some items that are essential whatever the project and others that are very useful. So make sure you have the following kit to hand.

**Craft knife** – essential for cutting long, straight edges; replace blades regularly to ensure a clean cut.

❀ Julie's Advice
*I recently started using a craft knife following a friend's advice, and it is so easy to use, so sharp and gives such good results. The blades are really easy to change too.*

**Cutting mat** – vital for use with a craft knife, to protect your work surface.

**Metal-edged ruler** – essential to use when cutting with a craft knife and also needed for measuring.

**Scissors** – keep the blades free from adhesive residue as well as sharp.

**Paper trimmer** – recommended for fast, accurate cutting (see opposite).

❀ Julie's Advice
*There are some tools that I just could not craft without, and my trimmers fall into this category. I have a large guillotine for bigger pieces of card and then my all-time favourite small trimmer, which has grid markings that help you cut to the right size.*

**Embossing tool** – use for scoring card (see opposite) and for curling paper and card (see page 19).

**Bone folder** – use to flatten folds in card to create a crisp, smooth finish.

**Japanese screw punch** – for making holes in card, chipboard, plasma and shrink plastic.

❀ Julie's Advice
*This is another tool I wouldn't be without. You can punch holes with it absolutely anywhere on your card or papercraft project in a variety of sizes – just brilliant!*

**Foam pads** – available in a variety of sizes; for mounting elements to card to give them a little depth.

**Craft glue** – for gluing papers and many embellishments such as flowers, punched shapes and crystals.

❀ Julie's Advice
*I always use a craft glue, as it is thicker and stronger than PVA (white) glue. I use a plastic bottle with a metal nib filled with the glue so that I can add very small amounts of glue to my work with its fine nozzle.*

**Double-sided tape** – invaluable for attaching elements (see page 112).

**Sewing machine** – for adding decorative stitched borders to paper and card elements.

❀ Julie's Advice
*I usually use a zigzag stitch to add interest to my cards rather than straight stitch, as it shows up the stitching more effectively and looks fabulous in light-catching metallic threads. Zigzag is also ideal for joining papers together, as you can stitch onto both papers easily.*

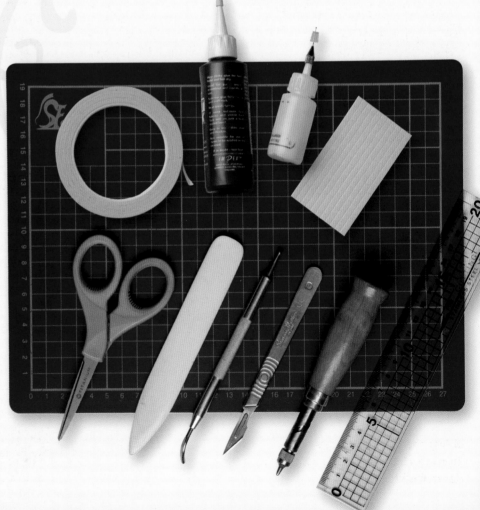

# BASIC TECHNIQUES

Follow these simple techniques to ensure that you always produce professional-looking cards and without expending extra time and effort. While pre-scored and folded cards, which are manufactured by machine, offer the best quality, you may prefer to buy your own card and cut it to size, to give you greater creative scope as well as to save on cost. Instructions are given here for cutting, scoring and folding for perfect results, together with useful advice on positioning and applying embellishments with double-sided tape, and guidance on creating patterned backgrounds and card inserts for adding special messages and decorating the insides of cards.

## CUTTING AND FOLDING YOUR OWN CARDS

The following steps show you how to achieve a clean, crisp-looking fold on both the inside and outside of all your cards.

**1** Cut your chosen card to the size you require using a paper trimmer. Alternatively, use a ruler and a craft knife on a cutting mat.

**2** Measure and mark on the card where you wish to make the fold. Place the card in the paper trimmer, lining the mark up with the groove that cuts the card. Starting at the top, pull an embossing tool down the groove to score the card. Alternatively, you can use a ruler with a bone folder held in an upright position.

**3** Align the edges of the card, then use a bone folder held flat to flatten the fold.

## SCOREBOARD

This item of equipment makes creating perfectly folded cards easy. Cut the card to size, then line up one edge with the raised edge on the scoreboard. Find the groove for the card size you want and score the card by dragging an embossing tool down the groove. Turn the card over, place one edge against the raised edge of the scoreboard and fold the card so that the two edges align perfectly.

### ❀ Julie's Advice
*Many people may think it's the other way around, but the indent on the crease of a fold is known as the 'valley' and the protruding part is known as the 'mountain'. The 'valley' is always on the outside of your card and the 'mountain' is always on the inside.*

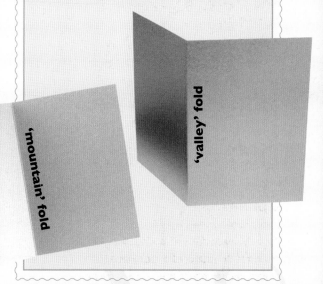

'mountain' fold

'valley' fold

# POSITIONING DESIGN ELEMENTS

It can be quite a challenge to position some elements correctly on a card – I have often ended up with lopsided designs that I have had to discard! But that was until I learned this clever technique from a print finisher, which allows you to move the element around until you have it perfectly placed before sticking it down.

**1** Attach double-sided tape to the edges of the element to be stuck to the main card. Then pull back just enough of the backing paper so that you can see the paper tabs from the front of the card. (If all the backing paper is removed, you only get one go at positioning.)

**2** Position the element on your card, moving it around until you are completely happy with its placement. Firm down where the tape is exposed.

**3** Carefully hold the element in the centre and pull the paper tabs off completely. Firm down on the card.

# CREATING FLORAL BACKGROUNDS

When you can't find exactly the right floral-patterned paper, or you can't get to the shops, here are a couple of crafty techniques for making your own floral-patterned papers using materials you are likely to have in your craft box as stencils.

### Punches
Punch a flower shape out of a piece of scrap card. Now take an inkpad and sponge and apply colour to the card through the aperture. Move it around the card, going on and off the card, to create a stunning background.

### Peel-off Stickers
Place a flower or flower-like peel-off sticker on the card, then sponge on ink to add colour just over the edges. Sponge gently and add soft touches of colour – you can add ink, but you can't take it away. Lift and move the sticker around the card, adding colour and going over the edges of the card.

*Other flower-like peel-off stickers, such as this snowflake, can be used in this way to create an interesting, stylized floral-type background design.*

# MAKING INSERTS

If you have added ribbons to the front of your card (see Fairy's Thank You, page 49), and for some aperture cards, you may wish to hide what is visible on the inside of the card. You may also want to add special messages or verses in your cards using a computer or stamp. Using an insert is a great solution in both cases; just remember, if using a computer, to print the message before cutting the paper to fit the card.

## COLOUR AND TEXTURE

Choose paper for your insert that will complement the card and the occasion. You may want to pick a colour to match your card, or achieve a subtle or bold contrast. Parchment-effect paper with a faint pattern gives a fantastic finish, and comes in many different colours. You can print onto vellum, which is available in many different colours, flecked with gold or silver, in an iridescent finish and even pearlized – perfect for special occasions, such as a wedding.

## EMBELLISHMENT

Use fancy-edged scissors to give added interest to your insert, or apply a gold, silver or coloured pen to the edge – or use a small inkpad – linking it to the cards' main colour theme. You don't want the insert to compete with the main design, so opt for a restrained decoration.

## ATTACHING THE INSERT

To attach the insert with double-sided tape, first cut the insert paper 6mm (¼in) smaller than the card all the way round. Fold in half and crease using a bone folder (see page 111). Apply double-sided tape to the back of the folded insert (see picture below), then place the insert into the folded card. Open the card from the back so that you can see the double-sided tape, then remove the backing paper. Shut the card, firming down along the fold of the card.

## DECORATING INSIDE

You can enhance your handcrafted cards yet further by selecting key elements of the design and using them on the inside – for instance, a panel of the same patterned paper used on the front, or a detail from the focal floral embellishment. See the Blossoming Ideas sections at the end of each chapter for some inspirational ideas, for example Buggy Bliss, page 109.

 Instead of using tape, tie the card and insert together at the centre fold using ribbon, thread or string decorated with beads, or punch two holes in the fold, thread ribbon through and tie.

# DECORATING AND MAKING ENVELOPES

There is a wide selection of ready-made envelopes available to buy in many different sizes, colours and finishes, from plain white to coloured, textured, pearlized, foiled and paper vellum. Whatever you choose, always make sure they are of good-quality – cheap, thin envelopes will detract from the look of your homemade card. However, if you have an unusually sized card, or want to create an envelope to coordinate with your card, you can make your own in a matter of minutes.

## PAPER

Always use paper for envelopes – about 120gsm is the right weight to score and fold for a professional finish, and will protect your creations if you are mailing them. As with inserts, the colour of the envelope can tone or contrast with the card. Patterned papers make great envelopes, but for cards that don't need much protection and are being hand-delivered, why not use pages from a gardening magazine or catalogue for instant, extra flower power!

## EMBELLISHMENTS AND LININGS

Before cutting out and making the envelope (see page 116 for an envelope template, or see the instructions opposite), you can stamp the paper with a motif or pattern to match the design on the card. Or you can adapt the techniques and motifs used for the card design to embellish the envelope – see the Blossoming Ideas sections at the end of each chapter for some specific examples, such as Winning Frame, page 68. You can also add a decorative lining to the envelope to coordinate with your card, either by stamping the reverse of the paper before cutting out the envelope or, for a ready-made envelope, stamping a separate piece of paper cut to fit inside the envelope, gluing it to the inside back and flap of the envelope and trimming around the flap (see Uplifting Spirit, page 48).

# MAKING AN ENVELOPE

Although most envelopes will be made from plain paper, the following steps show how paper vellum can be used instead to create a frosted envelope that allows the card inside to be seen. But you can use the instructions to make an envelope from any suitable paper to fit your card (see opposite). A homemade envelope can be as large as the size of the sheets of paper you can buy.

## YOU WILL NEED

- ❊ paper
- ❊ embossing tool (optional)
- ❊ bone folder
- ❊ pencil and ruler
- ❊ craft knife
- ❊ glue pen

**1** Lay your card in the centre of the sheet of paper vellum, or other paper, and fold the sides in, then the bottom up and lastly the top down, creasing the folds with a bone folder – if using paper other than vellum, score along the fold lines first using an embossing tool. Make sure that you allow enough for the bottom flap to fold up above the top flap.

**2** Unfold the paper and use a pencil and ruler to outline the envelope. Angle the sides of the bottom flap and the top of the top flap, as well as each end of the sides. Cut out the envelope using a craft knife.

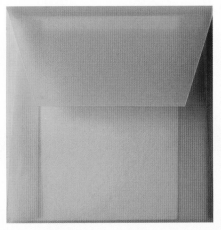

**3** Fold in the sides, then apply glue from the glue pen on the bottom flap to stick the envelope together.

**4** Once all the glue has dried, put the card inside the envelope and then use the glue pen along the top flap to seal the envelope.

# TEMPLATES

## WEDDING BANDS - BEAUTIFUL OUTSIDE, PAGE 29

**Envelope**

## INVITING ROSES, PAGES 80-83

**Heart**

# WELCOME BASKET, PAGES 100-103

**House**

To trace the envelope template start by copying the left hand side on page 116. Then move your paper over to page 117 and complete the envelope by matching up the tracing paper exactly with the edge of the template.

# MATERIALS

## CONTEMPORARY CHIC (PAGES 10–29)

### Tag Tonic (pages 14–15)
Square folded card – Alazen Green, scallop-top tag, crystals: Craftwork Cards
Fancy Pants Aged Florals Collection – Lovebird, paper flowers, ribbon: Hobby Horse Crafts

### Birthday Meadow (pages 16–19)
Square folded card – blue, Japanese screw punch: Craftwork Cards
Bazzill Bling card – Pink, Blue, Green: Crafts U Love
Basic Grey Papers – Gypsy Collection, Paper Shapers Whale of a Punch – Retro Daisy and Circle Punches: The Glitter Pot

### Daisy Patches (page 16)
9.9 x 21cm (4 x 8¼in) or DL folded card – white: Craftwork Cards
Bazzill Bling card – Pink, Blue, Green: Crafts U Love
Basic Grey Papers – Gypsy Collection, Paper Shapers Whale of a Punch – Retro Daisy and Circle Punches: The Glitter Pot

### 21st Birthday Bag (pages 20–23)
Pink and purple linen card, mini chipboard numbers, sheet of chipboard for base, crystals: Craftwork Cards
Pebbles Inc Paper Collection – Princess Flower and Stripe, Pebbles Inc Ribbon Collection – Raspberry, Doodle Bug rickrack – Lilac: The Glitter Pot
Quickutz flower and circle dies: Crafts U Love
Medium circle punch: Woodware

### Well Tagged (page 20)
Scallop-top tag card – hot pink, pink and purple linen card for die-cutting, crystals and glitter glue: Craftwork Cards
Pebbles Inc Paper Collection – Stripe, Pebbles Inc Ribbon Collection – Raspberry, Doodle Bug rickrack – Lilac: The Glitter Pot
Quickutz flower die: Crafts U Love
Cuttle Bug die-cutting system: Kars

### Seasonal Shimmer (pages 24–27)
Die-cut poinsettia, glitter glue, Japanese screw punch: Craftwork Cards
Bazzill Bling card – Ice Blue and Pink, ribbon: Crafts U Love
Silver metal sheet, decorative embossing roller, alcohol inks: LB Crafts
Cuttle Bug die-cutting system with embossing folder – Snowflakes: Kars
Nestabilities Scallop Circles: Once Upon a Stamp
CD tin: stationery stores

### Clearly Christmas (page 24)
Sheer Delights Scallop Circles, die-cut poinsettia, glitter glue: Craftwork Cards
Silver metal sheet, decorative embossing roller, alcohol inks, StazOn inkpad – White Opaque: LB Crafts
Cuttle Bug die-cutting system with embossing folder

– Snowflakes: Kars
Nestabilities Scallop Circles: Once Upon a Stamp
Bazzill Bling card – Pink, ribbon: Crafts U Love

### Easter Egg Trinity (page 28)
9.9 x 21cm (4 x 8¼in) or DL folded card – white linen, pink card, scallop-top tag, glitter glue: Craftwork Cards
Oval shape-cutter: Creative Memories
Pebbles Inc Paper Collection – My Baby Girl and Baby Pink Gingham, circle and flower punch: The Glitter Pot
Scallop-edged scissors, pink inkpad, ribbon: Crafts U Love

### Wedding Bands (page 29)
Acetate card, crystals, Japanese screw punch: Craftwork Cards
Pebbles Inc Paper Collection – Party Time Girl: The Glitter Pot
Flower punch – small and medium, paper flowers, ribbon: Hobby Horse Crafts
Corner rounder punch: Stampin Up

## FLORAL FAIRIES (PAGES 30–49)

### Birthday Girl's Fairytale (pages 34–35)
Scallop squares, Japanese screw punch, glitter glue, crystals: Craftwork Cards
Lilli of the Valley die-cut découpage sheets: Lilli of the Valley
Bazzill Bling card – Yellow and Orange, VersaMagic inkpad: Crafts U Love
Cuttle Bug die-cutting system and flower die: Kars Ribbon: Hobby Horse Crafts

### Festive Fairy (pages 36–39)
White textured card, scallop-top tag, crystals, glitter glue: Craftwork Cards
Françoise Read Fairy Delight rubber stamps: Woodware
Banana Frog Retro Snowflakes: Banana Frog
Daisy punches in different sizes, 22-gauge silver wire, ribbon: The Art of Crafts
Twinkling H20 paints, waterbrush, Brilliance inkpad, black permanent inkpad: The Glitter Pot

### Fairy Garland Tag (page 36)
Small scallop-top tag, purple card for punching: Craftwork Cards
Françoise Read Fairy Delight rubber stamps: Woodware
Twinkling H20 paints, waterbrush: The Glitter Pot
Daisy punch, ribbon: The Art of Crafts

### Daisy-chain Mobile (pages 40–43)
Card – Softies in Yellow and Pink, white sparkle paper, Tutti Frutti Paper Collection, fairy template, Peek a Boo Flowers, chipboard hanger and hearts, glitter glue: Craftwork Cards
Oval shape-cutter: Creative Memories
Flower and circle punches, ribbon: The Art of Crafts

### Hovering Hanger (page 40)
Chipboard door hanger, Softies card – Pink, Tutti Frutti Paper Collection, fairy template, Peek a Boo Flowers, glitter glue: Craftwork Cards
Flower and circle punches: The Art of Crafts

### Fairy's Secret Greetings (pages 44–47)
White sparkle paper for envelopes, white, pink and lilac card for tags, layering, die-cutting and stamping, crystals, glitter glue: Craftwork Cards
Envelope template: Stamp Addicts
Lavinia rubber stamps – Fairy, Toadstools, Flowers and Butterfly: Lavinia Stamps
Brilliance inkpads – Pink and Purple, black permanent inkpad, Quickutz die-cutting system with flower die, ribbon, glitter gel pens: Crafts U Love
Scoreboard, corner rounder punch, scallop circle punch and scallop-edged scissors: The Art of Crafts
Jewelled brads, ribbon: Hobby Horse Crafts

### Giant Gerbera Greeting (page 44)
21 x 14.8cm (8¼ x 5¾in) or C6 folded sparkle card – white, pink and white card for stamping and layering, glitter glue: Craftwork Cards
Lavinia rubber stamps – Fairy and Flowers: Lavinia Stamps
Brilliance inkpads – Pink, black permanent inkpad, ribbon, glitter gel pens: Crafts U Love
Nestabilities Scallop Circle and Circle: Once Upon a Stamp
Scallop-edged scissors: The Art of Crafts

### Uplifting Spirit (page 48)
Plasma flower-shaped card, crystals, glitter glue: Craftwork Cards
Françoise Read Fairy Delight clear rubber stamps – Flower Fairies: Woodware
Prima Flowers, black permanent inkpad, watercolour pencils: Hobby Horse Crafts

### Fairy's Thank You (page 49)
Square folded card – lilac, white card for stamping: Craftwork Cards
Françoise Read Fairy Delight clear rubber stamps – Flower Fairies: Woodware
Paper flowers, ribbon, jewelled brads: Hobby Horse Crafts
Black permanent inkpad, glitter gel pens: Crafts U Love

## FUNKY FLOWERS (PAGES 50–69)

### Flower-powered Success (pages 54–55)
Car-shaped card, crystals, glitter glue: Craftwork Cards
Daisy punches in difference sizes: The Art of Crafts
Bazzill Bling card – Blue, Pebbles Inc chalks: Crafts U Love

### Coming of Age Carnival (pages 56–59)
Acetate folded card, orange, pink and cherry card, glitter glue: Craftwork Cards
Cricut die-cutting system with George cartridge,

ribbons: Hobby Horse Crafts
Circle punches: The Art of Crafts

### Floral Bangle Tag (page 56)
Scallop-top tag, orange, pink and cherry card, glitter glue: Craftwork Cards
Cricut die-cutting system with George cartridge, ribbons: Hobby Horse Crafts
Pebbles Inc Paper Collection – Party Time Girl: The Glitter Pot

### Mother's Day Display (pages 60–63)
Large daisies, Retro Blooms, card in contrasting colours for flower centres, Japanese screw punch: Craftwork Cards
Dimensional Fluid, circle punches, ribbon: The Art of Crafts
Quickutz Die-cutting Squeeze with Goosebumps Circles: Crafts U Love
Drinking straws and vase: supermarket

### Geometric Greeting (page 60)
Large daisies, Retro Blooms, Cupcakes Paper Collection, square folded card – white, Oblong Ruffle: Craftwork Cards
Dimensional Fluid, circle and scallop circle punches, ribbon: The Art of Crafts
Quickutz Die-cutting Squeeze with Goosebumps Circles: Crafts U Love

### Forever Sweet 16 (pages 64–67)
30cm (12in) square canvas: general art store
Doodle Bug papers and brads: Crafts U Love
Chipboard numbers, glitter glue, crystals: Craftwork Cards
English Stamp Company Flower rubber stamp: English Stamp Company
Ultra Thick Embossing Powder, Acrylic Paint Dabbers: Art from the Heart
Flowers, buttons, embossing inkpad, ribbons: Hobby Horse Crafts

### Paisley Patchwork (page 64)
Square folded card – orange, crystals, glitter glue: Craftwork Cards
Doodle Bug papers and brads: Crafts U Love
Flowers, buttons, ribbons: Hobby Horse Crafts

### Winning Frame (page 68)
Square folded card – soft pink pearlescent, soft green pearlescent card, acetate frame, crystals: Craftwork Cards
Cuttle Bug die-cutting system with embossing folder – Stylized Flower: Kars
Ribbon and Soufflé Pens: Crafts U Love

### Christmas Candles (page 69)
Candle card, baubles, red and gold card, Japanese screw punch, glitter glue: Craftwork Cards
Stampin Up flower punch: Stampin Up
Pebbles Inc Chalks: Crafts U Love

### TRUE ROMANCE (PAGES 70–89)

### Wedding Lace Window (pages 74–75)
Square folded card – cream linen, cream linen card for punching, crystals, glitter glue: Craftwork Cards

Jumbo square and daisy punches in three sizes: The Art of Crafts

### Love-petals for Longing (pages 76–79)
Nine-square aperture card – gold shimmer, glitter glue, crystals: Craftwork Cards
Magenta Clear Stamps – Hearts: Woodware
VersaMagic inkpad – Pink, ribbon: Crafts U Love

### Singular Sentiment (page 76)
Tall, slim folded card – pink linen, tag template, crystals, glitter glue: Craftwork Cards
Magenta Clear Stamps – Hearts, inkpad: Woodware
VersaMagic inkpad – Pink, ribbon: Crafts U Love

### Inviting Roses (pages 80–83)
Secret centrefold card – cream, mini chipboard letters, crystals, glitter glue: Craftwork Cards
Pebbles Inc Paper Collection – My Girl Tiny Flower, Penny Black rubber stamp – Love Blush: The Glitter Pot
Nestabilities Circle and Scallop Circle: Once Upon a Stamp

### Beautiful Bouquet (page 80)
21 x 14.8cm (8¼ x 5¾in) or C6 folded sparkle card – white, Oblong Ruffle and Tile – Red, glitter glue: Craftwork Cards
Hero Arts rubber stamp – Delicate Rose Stems: The Glitter Pot
Watercolour pencils, ribbon: Hobby Horse Crafts

### Embossed Wedding Book (pages 84–87)
Chipboard squares, letters and mini numbers, accordion card – cream, gold pearlescent paper, embossed frames – Pretty Paisley, Perfect Petal Template 1 and 2, glitter glue: Craftwork Cards
Pebbles Inc Chalks, gold inkpad, ribbon: Crafts U Love
Basic Grey Paper Collection – Lollipop Shop/ Marzipan, circle punch: The Glitter Pot

### Perfectly Framed (page 84)
Chipboard squares and letters, Enchanted Paper Collection, card for inside cover, embossed frames – Julie's Daisy, Perfect Petal Template 2, glitter glue: Craftwork Cards
Pebbles Inc Chalks, ribbon: Crafts U Love

### Home Sweet Home (page 88)
House-shaped card, Winter Wonderland Paper Collection, card for windows and door, crystals, glitter glue: Craftwork Cards
Daisy punch, scallop oval punch, flower sequins: Hobby Horse Crafts
VersaMagic inkpads: Crafts U Love

### Number 1 Girl (page 89)
Scallop-top tag – hot pink, plasma number, Japanese screw punch, glitter glue: Craftwork Cards
English Stamp Company – Flower Stamp: English Flower Company
StazOn inkpad – White Opaque, ribbon: LB Crafts
Circle punch: Hobby House Crafts

### VINTAGE VOGUE (PAGES 90–109)

### Friendship Frieze (pages 94–95)
Square folded card – Softies Blue, Softies Blue card for layering, glitter glue, crystals: Craftwork Cards
Penny Black Stickers – When Birds Sing, brown inkpad: The Glitter Pot

### Laced with Love (pages 96–99)
Square folded card – Softies Cream: Craftwork Cards
Basic Grey Paper Collection – Infuse papers, Paper Shapers Whale of a Punch – Flower, buttons: The Glitter Pot
Bazzill Bling card, VersaMagic inkpad, ribbon: Crafts U Love
Corner rounder punch: Creative Memories
Sizzix paddle punch with heart die: The Craft Bug

### Antique Pouch (page 96)
21 x 14.8cm (8¼ x 5¾in) or C6 folded card – cream: Craftwork Cards
Basic Grey Paper Collection – Infuse papers, Paper Shapers Whale of a Punch – Flower, buttons: The Glitter Pot
Bazzill Bling card, VersaMagic inkpad: Crafts U Love

### Welcome Basket (page 100–103)
Enchanted Paper Collection – Teal, die-cut circles, brown paper, Perfect Petal Template 2, Japanese screw punch, glitter glue: Craftwork Cards
Scoreboard, ribbon: The Art of Crafts
VersaMagic inkpads: Crafts U Love

### Prettily Packaged (page 100)
Enchanted Paper Collection – Teal, Fancy Square Card Matt, crystals, glitter glue: Craftwork Cards
Paper flowers, ribbon: Hobby Horse Crafts

### Anniversary Announcement (pages 104–107)
Note Worthy Paper Collection – Making Memories, Bazzill Bling Flowers, Doodle Bug Glitter Brads, ribbon: Crafts U Love
30cm (12in) square chipboard sheet, chipboard hearts, sticky sheet, glitter glue: Craftwork Cards
Sizzix paddle punch with heart die: The Craft Bug

### Heartfelt Greetings (page 104)
Note Worthy Paper Collection – Making Memories, Doodle Bug Glitter Brads: Crafts U Love
Chipboard heart, glitter glue: Craftwork Cards

### Soothing Asymmetry (page 108)
21 x 9.9cm (8¼ x 4in) or DL folded card – green linen, crystals: Craftwork Cards
Basic Grey Paper Collection – LilyKate: The Glitter Pot
Doodle Bug Paper Frills: Crafts U love
Paper flowers: Hobby Horse Crafts

### Buggy Bliss (page 109)
Square folded card – pink linen, pink linen card for punching, crystals: Craftwork Cards
Basic Grey Paper Collection – LilyKate: The Glitter Pot
Frilled flower punch – medium and small, circle punches: The Art of Crafts

# SUPPLIERS

## UK SUPPLIERS

Art from the Heart
Studio 9
Hornbeam Park Avenue
Harrogate HG2 8QT
Tel: 01423 873 739
*www.afth.co.uk*

The Art of Crafts
101 Lynchford Road
North Camp
Farnborough
Hants GU14 6ET
Tel: 01252 377 677
*www.art-of-craft.co.uk*

Banana Frog
4 Loddon Road
Bourne End
Bucks SL8 5LT
Tel: 01628 533 066
*www.bananafrog.co.uk*

The Craft Bug
26 West View
Chirk
Wrexham LL14 5HN
Tel: 01691 774 778
*www.thecraftbug.co.uk*

Crafts U Love
Westcoats Farm
Charlwood
Horley
Surrey RH6 0ES
Tel: 01293 863 576
*www.craftsulove.co.uk*

Craftwork Cards Limited
Unit 2 The Moorings
Waterside Road
Stourton
Leeds LS10 1RW
Tel: 0113 276 5713
*www.craftworkcards.co.uk*

English Stamp Company
Worth Matravers
Dorset BH19 3JP
Tel: 01929 439 117
*www.englishstampcompany.com*

The Glitter Pot
Avery's Barn
Springfield Farm
Lewes Road
Scaynes Hill
West Sussex RH17 7NG
Tel: 01444 831 714
*www.theglitterpot.co.uk*

Hobby Horse Crafts
Gardens Cottage
33 Main Road
Elvaston
Derbyshire DE72 3EQ
Tel: 01332 572 904
*www.hobbyhorsecrafts.co.uk*

Lavinia Stamps
95 Park y Dre
Ruthin
Denbighshire LL15 1PH
Tel: 01824 702 057
*www.laviniastamps.co.uk*

LB Crafts
6 Rose Court
Market Place
Olney
Bucks MK46 4BY
Tel: 01234 714 848
*www.lbcrafts.com*

Lilli of the Valley
*www.lilliofthevalley.co.uk*

Once Upon a Stamp
6 Beetwell Street
Chesterfield
Derbyshire S40 1SH
Tel: 01246 278 448
*www.onceuponastamp.co.uk*

Stamp Addicts
Unit 5a Lyon Close
Woburn Road Industrial Estate
Kempston MK42 7SB
Tel:  01234 855 833
*www.stampaddictsshop.co.uk*

## UK DISTRIBUTORS

Kars
*www.kars.nl*

Woodware
Unit 2a Sandylands Business Park
Skipton
North Yorkshire BD23 2DE
Tel: 01756 700 024
*www.woodware.co.uk*

## US SUPPLIERS

Basic Grey
*www.basicgrey.com*

Bazzill Paper
*www.bazzillbasics.com*

Fancy Pants
*www.fancypantsdesigns.com*

Making Memories
*www.makingmemories.com*

Pebbles Inc
*www.pebblesinc.com*

Quickutz
*www.quickutz.com*

Stampin Up
*www.stampinup.com*

Ten Seconds Studio
*www.tensecondsstudio.com*

## ABOUT THE AUTHOR

Julie Hickey is a successful card-maker and papercafts tutor and author. She works with Sue, Richard and all the team at Craftwork Cards where she designs new products and is also involved with running the Craftwork Cards Card Club, a mail-order club that supplies projects, newsletters, inspiration and materials to their members all over the UK, USA and Europe.

Julie can often be found demonstrating at the major papercrafts, rubber stamping and scrapbooking shows up and down the UK. She is a regular contributor to many of the national craft magazines and has appeared on *Create and Craft* on Sky TV.

*Flower Power Papercrafts* will be Julie's fifth book, her third with David & Charles; both her previous books, *Quick & Clever Handmade Cards* and *Quick & Clever Instant Cards*, are bestsellers.

Julie lives in Horley, Surrey with her husband, Mervyn, and their two sons, Matthew and Owen.

# ACKNOWLEDGMENTS

***Mervyn, Matt and Owen*** Yet again you have all had to put up with so much mess, days with no food in the house, but most of all with the amount of time I have been in my 'shed'. I could not do it without all your love and support, so thank you. Special thanks for Matt for helping with the step-by-step note-taking.

***Mum*** You are always there for me, encouraging me and helping me in any way you can. Thank you for understanding just how much time and energy is taken up with the book.

***Sue and Rich*** A big thank you for all the gorgeous Craftwork Cards products that I have used throughout the book; your generosity in supplying me with whatever I need is much appreciated. Sue, you share so many of your creative ideas with me, which helps to spark new ideas for me – thank you. I also have to thank your amazing team at Craftwork Cards: Sonya, Michelle, Debbie, Rose, Steve, Simon and Ray. You all help me any way you can and make me feel so much a part of the team whenever I'm up at Leeds.

***Paula*** My little Spanish friend. I love the time we spend together and you are so generous in sharing your ideas and inspiration with me. Thank you.

***Jo*** You have been an absolute pleasure to work with; what you have turned my rough notes into is just amazing. Thank you so much for all your time and effort.

***Ginette*** Your photography is amazing. Your attention to detail has helped so much and the end result is quite simply stunning – again!

***Jenny, Charly, Beth, Emily and the team at David & Charles*** You have all be great to work with again, always there for any queries, full of encouragement, support and understanding. Thank you.

***Suppliers*** I want to thank all the shops that have helped with products for the projects (see opposite for details), with special thanks to the following people:

I was blown away by the generosity of Rachel and her mum Pam from Hobby Horse Crafts for the Cricut machine and all the other products you have helped me with. It is truly appreciated. Kars, for the Cuttle Bug die-cutting system and all the dies and embossing folders that you have so kindly supplied. Ada, you were so helpful and efficient sorting everything out for me so quickly.

Thank you to all the people who buy this book. I hope you enjoy it and pick it up when you need inspiration, and that the designs will spark creative ideas for you. Enjoy!

# INDEX

acetate 58–9, 68
anniversary card 98, 104–7

backgrounds, creating 112
bags 20–3, 100–3
birthday cards 16–19, 34–5, 44–7, 60, 98
   1st 89
   16th 64–7
   18th 56–9
   21st 20–3
booklet cards 44–7, 84–7
brads 8, 33, 73, 93, 104
buttons 53, 64, 73, 93

canvas 64
charms 53
Christmas cards 24–7, 36–9, 69
concertina fold 69, 84–7
congratulations card 68
contemporary chic 12–29, 118
crystals 13, 36, 54, 74, 109
cutting 7, 110, 111

daisies 9, 13, 32–3, 40, 74, 108
die-cutting 8, 9, 23, 26, 58
double-sided paper 6
double-sided tape 110, 112
driving test 54–5

Easter 28
embellishing 7, 8–9, 93
embossing 7, 27, 54, 63, 67, 68, 110
engagement 80–3, 116
envelopes 29, 48, 68, 88, 114–15, 116–17

fabric flowers 93, 96, 104, 108
floral fairies 32–49
flowers
   curling petals 19, 78, 103
   embellishing 9
   hand-made 8, 58–9, 62, 73, 87, 100
   paper 13, 33, 49, 93
   ready-made 8, 53, 73, 93
folding 110, 111
friendship card 94–5
funky flowers 52–69, 118–19

gerbera 44
get well card 14–15, 48
gifts 49, 94, 100
girl's birthday 34–5, 44–7, 60, 89
glitter 7
glue 110

hydrangeas 73, 93

inserts 113

materials 118–20
mobile, daisy-chain 40–3
Mother's Day 60–3

new baby 109
new home 88, 100–3, 117
notice board 104–7

paper, choosing 6–7

pens, specialist 7
poinsettias 9, 24–7, 69
positioning elements 112
punches 6, 8, 59, 110, 112

quilling 73

ribbon 8, 13, 33, 53, 63, 73, 93, 99, 113
romantic cards 72–89, 96–9, 119
roses 9, 80–3

sequins 13
stencils 112
stickers, peel-off 94, 112
stitching 19, 53, 66, 110
sympathy card 76, 108

tags 14–15, 20–1, 28, 36, 56, 89, 96
tearing 7
techniques 111–13
templates 116–17
thank you cards 16, 48, 49, 98
thinking of you card 76
tools 110

Valentines Day 96–9
vintage vogue 92–109, 119

weddings 29, 74–5, 84–7, 100, 116–17
weight of paper 7